T0077885

Born to Sweet Delight

Life Affirmed,
Fate Defied

JOHN BARRY FORSYTH

WESTBOW
P R E S S®
A DIVISION OF THOMAS NELSON
& ZONDERVAN

[Scripture quotations are from] New Revised Standard Version Bible, copyright © 1989 National Council of the Churches of Christ in the United States of America. Used by permission. All rights reserved worldwide.

Scripture quotations taken from the New English Bible, copyright © Cambridge University Press and Oxford University Press 1961, 1970. All rights reserved.

Scripture taken from the New King James Version®. Copyright © 1982 by Thomas Nelson. Used by permission. All rights reserved.

Passages marked "KJV" are taken from the King James Bible.

WestBow Press books may be ordered through booksellers or by contacting:

WestBow Press
A Division of Thomas Nelson & Zondervan
1663 Liberty Drive
Bloomington, IN 47403
www.westbowpress.com
1 (866) 928-1240

ISBN: 978-1-9736-0925-4 (sc)
ISBN: 978-1-9736-0926-1 (hc)
ISBN: 978-1-9736-0924-7 (e)

Library of Congress Control Number: 2017918061

Print information available on the last page.

WestBow Press rev. date: 11/20/2017

John Barry Forsyth is an ordained Presbyterian Minister.
He has served congregations in British Columbia,
Ontario, Nova Scotia, and Quebec in Canada.
John Barry has degrees in history, education, and theology.
At various times, he has been a teacher, counsellor,
triathlete, and competitive swimmer.

CONTENTS

FOREWORD

Certain patriarchs and matriarchs, poets and sages, lovers and apostles, slaves and hymn writers, prisoners and pilgrims make their contribution to this volume. Their lives were taken up with journeys of faith and passages of profound significance for them and many others. They struggled bravely against oppression and refused to surrender. They were ordinary men and women of complex emotion and conflicting thought. Yet, their movement was always forward to a welcoming God, The One who had in some way or another always been with them. In whatever circumstance they found themselves, they had an enduring smile in their hearts if not on their faces. They affirmed life and defied fate.

Within these pages, you will find encouragement for your faith, biblical exposition from the Old Testament Scriptures – with reference points to the New Testament, stories of journey and song, sagas of struggle and resolution, chronicles of courage and caring, and histories of divine intervention, all of them measured against an infinite glory and the weigh-scales of delight.

John Barry Forsyth

One

HOLD INFINITY IN YOUR HAND
Wm. Blake

Every Morn & every Night
Some are born to sweet delight.
God appears & God is Light
To those poor Souls who dwell in Night,
But does a Human Form Display
To those who Dwell in Realms of Day.

(Wm. Blake, *Auguries of Innocence*)

"Trust in the Lord, and do good; so shalt thou dwell in the land, and verily thou shalt be fed. Delight thyself also in the Lord; and he shall give Thee the desires of thine heart. Commit thy way unto the Lord; trust also in him; and he shall bring it to pass. And he shall bring forth thy righteousness as the light, and thy judgment as the noonday."

(Psalm 37:3-6, King James Version)

To see a world in a grain of sand,
And a heaven in a wild flower,
Hold infinity in the palm of your hand,
And eternity in an hour.
(*College Survey*, pg. 668)

These are the opening lines of William Blake's famous poem, *Auguries of Innocence*. William Blake was born in 1757 and died in 1827. From his earliest days, Blake was greatly aware of the presence of God indwelling and surrounding all things. An awareness of the divine presence illumined and emboldened his entire life. His brilliant mind and inquiring spirit sensed the spiritual significance in and with everything.

William Blake began to write poetry at the age of twelve. Over the course of his entire life, he produced some of the finest poetry in the English language. Blake was not highly educated nor was he born into wealth or circumstance. Nevertheless, his insights, wisdom and mystical awareness were deep, profound, and penetrating in a most remarkable and unique way. It has been said of William Blake that he was caught up into levels of being to which few of us penetrate. His wife once said, "I have very little of Mr. Blake's company. He is always in Paradise." (College *Survey*, pg. 662)

We have this summary of his William Blake's remarkable abilities and singular perceptions:

> Blake taught himself, beating out the lonely path of an
> original genius. He came to regard the world of the senses
> as a tapestry woven full of symbols, a mine of metaphors,
> in which every object and event points beyond itself to a
> transcendent meaning. (*Survey*, pg. 661)

In 1809, when Blake was fifty-two years old, an exhibition of his paintings was a complete failure. The prophetic message in his writings was seldom grasped and understood. He was struggling with poverty and a lack of recognition. Yet, he was able to speak these words to a pretty, society girl at a party, "May God make this world to you, my child, as beautiful as it has been to me." Here is the account of their meeting:

> She thought it strange that such a poor, worn man, dressed in shabby clothes, could imagine the world to be beautiful to him – nursed as she was in all the elegance and luxury of wealth. In later years, she understood what Blake meant and treasured the few words he had spoken to her. (Wm. Blake, *Everyman's Poetry*. pg xix)

Blake's final demise is described this way:

> After seventy years of obscure, toilsome, impoverished, solitary, and greatly joyous life he died almost unknown uttering cheerful songs to his Maker. (*Survey*, pg.662)

On the last day of his life he composed and uttered songs to his Maker, saying to his wife, "My beloved, they are not mine – no – they are not mine." (Wm. Blake, *Everymans Poetry*. pg.vii)

Here are the closing lines of Auguries of Innocence (certain words are capitalized for emphasis: Soul, God, Light, Night, Human Form, and Day):

> Every night and every morn
> Some to misery are born.
> Every morn and every night
> Some are born to sweet delight.
> Some are born to sweet delight,
> Some are born to endless night.
> We are led to believe a lie
> When we see not through the eye,
> Which were born in a night, to perish in a night,
> When the Soul slept in beams of light.
> God appears and God is Light,
> To those poor souls who dwell in Night,
> But does a Human Form display
> To those who dwell in realms of Day.
> (*Survey*, pg.669)

In Paul the Apostle's second letter to the church at Corinth, he introduces the subject of mystical and ecstatic experiences. Paul, like William Blake much later on, had certain transcendent experiences which transported him into "the heavenly realms" and gave him particular insights and special knowledge of spiritual matters. Paul began his treatment of the subject with this statement:

> "I will go on to visions and revelations in the Lord. I know a person in Christ who fourteen years ago was caught up to the third heaven - whether in the body or out of the body I do not know; God knows." (12:1, 2)

The apostle Paul was answering a challenge which was being presented to him by some rival Christian leaders who questioned his authority and his credentials. In effect, his challenge to them could be expressed this way, "What visions can you claim to have had as authority for your ministry? You say that you are apostles. What revelations have you received from God to authenticate your claims?"

Paul's reply is curious. He was unwilling to identify himself as the person whom he speaks of as having visions and revelations. Thus he writes, "I know a person." (12:2). As we study the passage, it is obvious that Paul is referring to himself. But, he does so in a manner which is impersonal. He uses the third person instead of the first person. The apostle says that he was "caught up to the third heaven." (12:2). But, he doesn't give any details about the place of the body in such an experience:

> "Whether in the body or out of the body I do not know, God knows." (12:3)

Certain persons at that time claimed to have been lifted out of the body during intense, ecstatic experiences. Paul made no such claim. He was not interested in defining his experiences in such a dramatic, perhaps self-serving way. It was enough for him to simply say, "God knows."

Paul's particular ecstatic experience was remarkable, to be sure. He tells us that it happened fourteen years ago. (12:2). In the meantime, he did have other mystical, visionary encounters. Most notable, of course, was his vision of the risen Christ, on the road to Damascus which resulted in his conversion. As Paul journeyed, suddenly a light shone around him from heaven. He fell to the ground as Jesus himself spoke to him: "Why do you persecute me?" Jesus asked. (Acts 9:4)

Later on, when Paul was preaching the gospel in Asia Minor, he received a vision which called him to take the message of Christ to Macedonia. The incident is recorded in Acts 16:9:

> A vision appeared to Paul in the night. A man of Macedonia stood and pleaded with him, saying, "Come over to Macedonia and help us."

Earlier on, when Paul had been in Corinth, he received a vision which gave him confidence that he would be blessed and protected in that place:

> Now the Lord spoke to Paul in the night by a vision, "Do not be afraid but speak, and do not keep silent; for I am with you, and no one will attack you to hurt you; for I have many people in this city." (Acts 18: 9, 10)

Returning to the passage in 2 Corinthians 12, we discover that while Paul had ecstatic experiences, visions, and revelations, he did not wish to boast about them. As he had already said, in verse 1: "It is necessary to boast" (that is, at least, to speak of it) but, nothing is to be gained by it." In verse 4, we are told, that:

> [Paul] was caught up into Paradise and heard things that are not to be told, that no mortal is permitted to speak.

Paul's experiences took him to the highest possible heights of spiritual ecstasy. They were greatly mystical and transcendent. They were beyond imagining and entirely unique. However, Paul insists that such ecstatic experiences, while valuable in certain ways, are not worthy of the greatest attention or the highest honour:

"On my own behalf, I will not boast, except of my weaknesses. I refrain from it, so that no one may think better of me than what is seen in me or heard in me, even considering the exceptional character of the revelations." (vs. 5, 6)

The apostle then goes on to describe "a thorn in the flesh." It was a serious, physical affliction of some kind which kept him from exalting himself overmuch:

"To keep me from being too elated, a thorn in the flesh was given to me, to keep me from being too elated." (vs.7)

Paul prayed to God three times as he pleaded with God to take away his affliction. Each time the answer was given:

"My grace is sufficient for you, for my strength is made perfect in weakness." (vs.9, KJV)

Paul's conclusion is this:

"I will boast all the more gladly of my weaknesses, so that the power of Christ may dwell in me." (vs.9)

The final resolution is given:

"I am content with weaknesses, insults, hardships, persecutions, and calamities for the sake of Christ; for whenever I am weak, then I am strong." (12:10).

To see a world in a grain of sand
And a heaven in a wild flower,
Hold infinity in the palm of your hand,
And eternity in an hour.
(Blake, *Auguries*)

How will we see the world? What visions of sweet delights will dance before our eyes? Do we see evidences of heaven all around us? Will infinity, that which is unlimited, break open for us that which finite and limited? Can we experience "eternity in an hour" and, that which lasts forever, in one "delight-full" moment?

At one dramatic point in his public ministry, a woman who had been caught in the act of adultery was brought before Jesus. The scribes and Pharisees, who had brought the woman forward, wanted her to be stoned to death, in accordance with the law of Moses. They asked Jesus what should be done with such a sinner as her. He stooped down and wrote something on the ground. Jesus pretended that he had not heard them. They pressed him to give them an answer. Jesus stood up and said: "He who is without sin among you, let him cast the first stone." (John 8:7, KJV)

Everyone who was there left the scene. Jesus was left alone with the woman. She called him "Lord," as she acknowledged that no one was present anymore to condemn her. Jesus then said: "Neither do I condemn you, go and sin no more." (8:11, KJV). In addition, Jesus spoke these words: "I am the light of the world. Whoever follows me will never walk in darkness but will have the light of life." (8:12).

We are led to believe a lie,
When we see not through the eye.
(Blake, *Auguries*)

The eye which beholds the Christ of God in his glory as the Light of the world cannot consign another person to an unjust punishment. The eye which delights to see visions of "the heavenly realms" cannot condemn another to the darkness of death. The eye which has seen untold mysteries at the highest levels of human experience cannot direct stones towards brothers and sisters who have become disadvantaged and made to be vulnerable.

We are "born to sweet delight" when Jesus Christ appears before us, summoning us to follow him - for all our days and time on this earth. Our souls sleep under "beams of light" as the power of the risen Easter Christ stands guard over our tombs. That which is finite is taken up into the infinite. That which is bound by time is released into the place of timelessness. Paul, the visionary apostle, gives us this summary of what is the ultimate transcendent experience with which there is no greater delight:

> Behold, I show you a mystery; we shall not all sleep, but we shall all be changed, the dead shall be raised incorruptible. This corruptible (body) must put on incorruption, and this mortal [body] must put on immortality. (1Corinthians 15: 51-53, KJV)

God appears, and God is Light,
To those poor souls who dwell in Night.
(Blake, *Auguries*)

There is no one to condemn us anymore. They have all been rendered speechless. They have all departed. Nor do we condemn ourselves anymore, because we have heard God say to us: "My grace is sufficient for you: for my strength is made perfect in weakness." (2 Corinthians 12:9 KJV)

A "Human Form" of God has appeared. We behold his glory: "... as of the only begotten of the Father, full of grace and truth." (John 1:14, KJV). Truly, it is possible for us to dwell in "realms of day." It is our destiny to be "lifted up" out of ourselves; out from our sins; out from our weaknesses. The "Light of life" surrounds, enlivens, and emboldens us. It transports us to the highest heights. At times, we are ecstatic with sweet delight and joy inexpressible. But, we must not give ourselves over to boasting. That which we experience has been given to us. We have not crafted, invented, or concocted it ourselves. We have simply received it in the unique calling and destiny which has come to us from above.

Two

DEAREST FRESHNESS
DEEP DOWN
Creation

God is a God!

God is a God!
God don't never change!
God is a God,
And He always will be God!
 He made the sun to shine by day,
 He made the sun to show the way,
 He made the stars to show their light,
 He made the moon to shine by night, saying –
God is a God!
God don't never change!
God is a God,
And He will always be God!
 The Earth's his footstool and Heaven's His throne;
 The whole creation, all His own;
 His love and power will prevail,
 His promises will never fail, saying –
God is a God!
God don't never change!
God is a God,
And He will always be God.
(Traditional African American Spiritual)

In 1918, at the close of World War 1, Gerald Manley Hopkins wrote a poem which extolled the beauty of nature over against the background of chaos and destruction engendered by the war. The title of the poem is, *God's Grandeur.*

> The world is charged with the grandeur of God.
> It will flame out, like shining from shook foil;
> It gathers to a greatness, like the ooze of oil
> Crushed. Why do men then now not reck his rod?
> Generations have trod, have trod, have trod;
> And all is seared with trade; bleared, smeared with toil;
> And wears man's smudge and shares man's smell:
> The soil, is bare now, nor can foot feel, being shod.
> And for all of this, nature is never spent;
> There lives the dearest freshness deep down things;
> And though the last lights off the black West went
> Oh, morning, at the brown brink eastward, springs;
> Because the Holy Ghost over the bent
> World broods with warm breast and with ah! bright wings.
> (*Modern Poetry,* pg. 31)

We wonder how Hopkins could still recognize the "grandeur of God" in nature when the devastation of war was so much in evidence at that time. He insists that the power and beauty of God's creative order "flames out" unrestrained in its spread, everywhere shining in splendor.

Hopkins concludes that "nature is never spent." In spite of what humankind has done to the natural landscape with the ravages of bombs, tanks, soldiers, and armaments, nature is not wearied or worn out as it recovers from the devastation it has experienced. There is a "dearest freshness deep down" within creation - it lives, survives, and thrives because it is inextricably linked with the original order of things. Nature can be devastated but not destroyed.

The poet paints a vivid picture of the adverse effects of industrial development, empire building commerce, and mankind's proud toil:

And all is seared with trade; bleared, smeared with toil;
And wears man's smudge and shares man's smell:
The soil, is bare now, nor can foot feel, being shod.

In the summer time, we like to take our shoes off and walk barefoot along the sandy beaches of a pond, lake, or ocean. We have a carefree feeling when our feet are "un-shod." But, rising ocean waters will soon obliterate many beaches. The glaciers in the Polar Regions are melting at an alarming rate. Our feet will not be able to feel the earth the same way.

The "smudge and smell" of mankind is evident everywhere. The environment is not being adequately nurtured, protected, or safeguarded from harm. We wonder if nature will be able to withstand the crippling onslaughts of pollution, wasteful practices, the crass exploitation of its resources, and, the sinister shearing of its landscapes.

Our earth is becoming drab grey in colour. How much time is left for our "green earth?" How soon will it be before we see "the last lights off the black West?"

In Genesis, the holy book of origins, we read this:

> And God said, "Let the waters under the sky be gathered together into one place, and let the dry land appear." And it was so. God called the dry land Earth, and the waters that were gathered together he called Seas. And God saw that it was good. (1: 9)

The primeval waters were gathered together and the dry land appeared having been separated out from the waters. The Jerusalem Bible translates the Hebrew somewhat differently: "God said, 'Let the waters under heaven come together into a single mass.'"

Creation came into being – it began its existence, because, God spoke a mighty word. As the command of God reverberated over all that then was a space was created by God "outside Himself." This separated out space became the container for creation as we know it. In that God is the supreme craftsman for all that is, creation reflects his divine image. Creation has been called, "the theater of God's glory and action." God spoke, acted, and power was imparted - "And it was so." God spoke, acted, and glory was transmitted "And it was so." God spoke his mighty word and light and goodness from God emanated out over and around the entire universe. Every galaxy, star, planet, and moon were inundated and infused with the divine image.

Kabbalah is the term used to designate and describe the Jewish mystical tradition. Within its teachings there are symbols, allusions, and multiple levels of meaning which have attracted readers for centuries. Basically, it is traditional wisdom received and treasured from the past. Its primary aspects include the radical transcendence of God and lofty attempts to define the divine attributes.

Here is a fascinating quote which ponders the question of creation:

> If God pervades all space, how was there room for anything other than God to come into being? The first divine act is thought to be not emanation, but withdrawal. God withdrew his presence "from itself to itself," withdrawing in all directions away from one point at the center of its infinity, thereby creating a vacuum. This vacuum served as the site of creation. Into the vacuum, God emanated a ray of light. (*The Essential Kabbalah*, pg. 15)

The book of Genesis puts its focus on the first great emanation of light bringing form out of formlessness - "that which is" being created out from nothing this way:

> In the beginning when God created the heavens and the earth the earth was a formless void and darkness covered the face of the deep, while a wind from God swept over the face of the waters. Then God said, "Let there be light"; and there was light.

> And God saw that the light was good; and God separated the light from the darkness. God called the light Day, and

the darkness he called Night. And there was evening and there was morning, the first day. (1:1-4)

In the New Testament, the mighty Word of God spoken at creation is drawn into a tight connection with Jesus Christ. The gospel of John, chapter 1, verses 1-3:

> In the beginning was the Word, and the Word was with God, and the Word was God. The same was in the beginning with God. All things were made by him; and without him was not any thing made that was made. (King James translation)

Jesus Christ is the Word of God incarnate, that is – The Word "become flesh." As a man among men, the one born in Bethlehem, the one who grew up in Nazareth, Jesus was human "Yes! very much so!" But, he was also divine – having come out from God. The Apostle John proclaims the marvelous truth and mystery that Jesus was with God when Creation was being accomplished. He was "in the beginning" with God, before all else came into being. Dr. Leon Morris, the commentator, writes:

> There never was a time when the Word (that is Jesus) was not. There never was a thing which did not depend on him for its very existence. (*New International Commentary*, John, pg.73)

Jesus was therefore, pre-existent. He existed before Creation. He is also Co-creator – active in bringing creation into being, along with the Father and the Holy Spirit. The Father created but he did it through The Word which in the Holy Spirit, as we are told in Genesis 1:2 "swept over the face of the waters."

We affirm these mysteries defined and explicated in the Bible with a sense of wonder and awe. They define our understanding of the universe and of the earth which is our home. They help us to have respect for creation and all peoples who dwell upon the earth. They invigorate and inspire us to "charge the world – with our grandeur," borrowing some of Gerald Manley Hopkin's poetic words. Made in the image of God, "the Imago Dei," we reflect God's glory when we live creatively charged lives of goodness, mercy, love and compassion. Our lives are essentially a gift from God. We do not choose to be born. We are given life. It comes from beyond – out of the mystery and wonder of God's being, purpose, and eternal will. It also touches what is incredibly near as God infuses everything with life, vitality, and divine presence.

The Apostle Paul gave enlightened instruction to the Greeks of Athens, Greece – as to the nature of these things:

> The God who made the world and everything in it, he who is Lord of heaven and earth, does not live in shrines made by human hands, nor is he served by human hands, as though he needed anything, since he himself gives to all mortals life and breath and all things. From one ancestor he made all nations to inhabit the whole earth, and he allotted the times of their existence and the boundaries of the places where they would live, so that they would search for God and perhaps grope for him and find him – though indeed he is not far from each one of us. For "In him we live and move and have our being;" as even some of your poets have said, "For we too are his offspring." (Acts 17:24-28)

The earth which is our home is also a wondrous gift from God. The American theologian, Matthew Fox, highlights this "giftedness" as he relates the creation of the world to a lineage of cosmic gift giving:

> In the beginning was the gift.
> And the gift was with God and the gift was God.
> And the gift came and set its tent among us,
> first in the form of a fireball
> that burned unabated.
> Gifts upon gifts, birthing gifts exploding,

imploding, gifts of light, gifts of darkness.
Cosmic gifts in a vast secret of a plan.
(*Creation Spirituality*, Prologue, pg. 1)

If we view life and the world as a gift we will be thankful for everything. We will wake up in the morning with a song of praise upon our lips. If life is conceptualized as something given from beyond which has come close we will be conscious of the transcendent presence of the divine surrounding us. We will be constantly attuned to and continually aware of the presence of the Spirit of God permeating all of Creation.

In one of his prayers, George MacLeod, founder of the Iona Community in Scotland, speaks of the presence of God as "warming and moving all creation." Furthermore, in the poem, *The Whole Earth Shall Cry Glory*, he writes:

> Invisible we see you,…
> In you all things consist and hang together.
> The very atom is light energy,
> the grass is vibrant,
> the rocks pulsate.
> All is in flux;
> turn but a stone and an angel moves.
> (*Iona Prayers*, Wild Goose Publications)

There is an infinite glory to be found in creation simply because the Creator of all things is infinitely wonderful and glorious. We need only look around us at any moment and our minds are overwhelmed with the wonders we behold.

There is an infinite glory to be found in our Saviour, Jesus Christ, whom we extol with the ancients as indeed "the fairest of ten thousand, the lily of the valley, the bright and morning star."

The Apostle John reminds us of the giftedness and unadulterated goodness that is to be found in Christ's coming from heaven: "God so loved the world that He gave his only begotten Son that whosoever believes in Him should not perish but have everlasting life." (John 3:16)

Our lives reflect the radiance of God as Jesus Christ lives his life in us. The "grandeur of God" takes up residence in us as we humbly do "all that we do" to the glory of God.

The Westminster Catechism gives us time honoured instruction as to what constitutes our fundamental "chief end" and purpose in life:

Question 1. What is the chief end of man?

Answer – Man's chief end is to glorify God and enjoy Him for ever. (*Confession of Faith*, pg. 115)

Three

DEPARTURE INTO
THE UNKNOWN
Abraham

THE WAYFARING STRANGER (1784)

The Wayfaring Stranger, dated 1784, was a traditional spiritual often sung by the pioneers that inhabited the southern Appalachian Mountains and typically used at revival meetings. The pioneers lived grueling lives full of hardships and trials and anticipated eternity with an expectancy that is expressed beautifully in the words of the song that talks of both the struggles and blessed paradise "over Jordan" (the river).

I'm just a poor, wayfaring stranger
A-trav,lin' through this world of woe,
But there's no sickness, toil or danger
In that bright land to which I go.

I'm goin' there to see my mother;
I'm goin' there, no more to roam.
I'm just a-goin' over Jordan,
I'm just a-goin'over home.

My father lived and died a farmer
A-reapin' less than he did sow.
And now I follow in his footsteps.
A'knowin' less than he did know.

I'm goin' there to see my father;
I'm goin' there, no more to roam.
I'm just a-goin' over Jordan,
I'm just a -goin' over home.

I know dark clouds will gather round me.
My way is steep and rough, I know,
But fertile fields lie just before me
In the fair land to which I go.

I'm goin' there to see my brother;
I'm goin' there no more to roam.
I'm just a-goin' over Jordan,
I'm just a-goin' over home.

"Go From Your Country"

In the first chapters of Genesis, in the Old Testament, we have the story of creation. The heavens and the earth, the plants, and the animals, are all created by God. The final, great creative act of God is to create human beings. The first humans, Adam and Eve, make their appearance upon the earth. They are placed in a garden paradise, but before long, are tempted by Satan and fall into sin. They are then banished from the garden called Eden.

One of the sons of Adam and Eve, Cain, commits the first murder as he kills his brother Abel. The descendants of the first man and woman become increasingly wicked. God decides that he must destroy the earth. Great rains fall upon the earth – entirely flooding it. Everyone on the face of the earth perishes except Noah and his family. They are saved in the ark which God had instructed Noah to build.

The human race continues after the flood. But once again, the wickedness of humans increases. The tower of Babel is built as a symbol of defiance against God. The Lord's wrath is kindled a second time, and a swift and fierce judgment is executed by the Almighty. The peoples of the earth are quickly scattered in all directions. The unity of the human race is completely lost as individual nations and language groups move away from a common centre.

No indication is given that a restoration of humankind will take place. There is no "word of grace" given in the situation. Questions arise. "Has God's patience and forbearance reached its final limit? Is there any hope for the human race, now so divided and broken apart? What will the Lord do next? Will the descendants of Adam and Eve be given another chance to make something good of themselves?"

What follows in Genesis, chapter 12, is the election and blessing of Abraham. The first great patriarch "father of all the faithful" is chosen by God for an eternal blessing. Primeval history comes to an end with Abraham. Genesis, chapter 12, is an important junction point in the history of salvation. In Abraham, the covenant promise that God will provide a way of salvation for all peoples is first clearly presented. With Abraham, we learn that one man, one person, can know God – and, in that delightful knowing, there can be great blessing for countless others.

> Now the Lord said to Abram, "Go from your country and your kindred and your father's house to the land that I will show you. I will make of you a great nation, and I will bless you, and make your name great, so that you will be a blessing. In you all the families of the earth shall be blessed." (12: 1-3)

Abraham was called by God to leave his father's house, the place of his birth, origins, and heritage. He was called by God to make a radical break from his past. He was called to leave everything which was familiar to him – family and friends, hearth and home. Abraham was told by God that he must make a journey – a journey into an unknown land and an unfamiliar place. But, God would show the way. The sovereign Lord of all time and history was going to provide an altogether new beginning for humankind. Great blessing was going to come into the entire world because of Abraham's "going out from his father's house."

In his commentary on the book of Genesis, Gerhard Von Rad, offers these insights:

> With Abraham, the particularism of election begins. From the multitude of nations, God chooses a man, pulls him away from his family, and tribal ties, and makes him the father of a new nation: and, the recipient of great promises of salvation. What is promised to Abraham has universal meaning for all generations on earth. (pg.154)

The Lord said to Abraham, "Go from your country – to a land that I will show you."

It's not easy for anyone to move away from their "land of origin," the places where they grew up – the places they call "home." But, many people do accomplish such a move. As the faithful of God move away from their ancestral homes and places of origin, they perpetuate the faithfulness of Abraham, the father of all those who embrace, and confess the promises of God. In the book of Hebrews, they are called "strangers and pilgrims upon the earth." (11:13, KJV)

Clearly, a large majority of us are immigrants to this great land of Canada. We have come recently, or else are the descendants – the "sons and daughters" of immigrants from a previous time. We have either received the call ourselves, or inherited it from our ancestors. "Go from your country to the land of Canada, which I will show to you. It is there that I will give you a great blessing, you and your descendants after you."

My grandparents, on my mother's side, came to Canada from England in the early 1920's. Richard Harry and Bertha Mary Willmott settled near Victoria, British Columbia – happy to be in a new land, in an altogether new place. But, the pull of "the old country" remained strong with them. They were happy in their new location, but they felt a strong desire to return to England.

In 1931, they left Vancouver Island and journeyed across Canada by train. My mother Irene and my aunt Betty, young girls at the time, were with them. They boarded a ship and crossed the Atlantic in order to be reunited with their family and friends. It was a long, arduous trip for a family of four. They stayed in England for six months, fully expecting that they had said goodbye to Canada forever.

My grandparents had been homesick for England, and had returned to stay permanently. But, England had changed and they had changed. It was a difficult decision, but, they decided to return to Canada. They made their way back to Vancouver Island and never left again.

"Go from your country to a land that I will show you. Go!
You will be homesick. Go! You will want to return. Go!
You will be happy in your new place, but it will not be easy.
Go, and I will be with you!"

As with Abraham of old, God speaks to us, and says, "You must stay in the land that I will show you, and never return from whence you have come. Your heart will always ache for the old places, the old country, but you must stay in the place to which I have called you."

In the New Testament, in the book of Hebrews, believers in Jesus Christ are reminded that they are sons and daughters of Father Abraham. They are the descendants of the first great patriarch who obeyed God and became a sojourner in the land of promise.

By faith Abraham obeyed when he was called to go out to the place which he would receive as an inheritance. He went out, not knowing where he was going, and he dwelt in the land of promise. He waited for the city whose builder and maker is God. (11:8-10, NKJV)

The journey to the land of promise is a challenging journey - away from everything which is familiar. It is a movement out of, and away from, "our father's house." Often, it is a great distance away - though not always in miles and kilometers. The distances traversed are through wilderness stretches of the psyche, desert areas in the soul, and tortuous paths of the mind. People of faith must, therefore, travel light and travel hard if they expect to reach their chosen destination. As strangers and pilgrims entering previously unexplored territory "we have no continuing city, but seek the one to come." (Hebrews 13:14)

In the life of faith, there is constant movement forward. The author of the book of Hebrews tells his readers that they are "partners in a heavenly call." (3:1). In chapter 6, verses 4 and 5, he states that it is impossible for them to fall away because they have been enlightened:

> We have tasted the heavenly gift, and have shared in the
> Holy Spirit, and have tasted the goodness of the word of
> God and the powers of the age to come.

There is, therefore, no permanent place for those who have received the heavenly call wherein we may dwell. We are constantly moving through time towards the end of our days. Our continual focus is thus towards heaven. Our calling is upwards - towards our final home. Our faith is linked to "the city which is yet to come" in the heavenly, eternal kingdom of Christ.

The Apostle John's vision of the city which is to come is recorded in the book of Revelation:

> "Then I saw a new heaven and a new earth; for the first heaven and the first earth had passed away. And I saw the holy city, the new Jerusalem, coming down out of heaven from God, prepared as a bride adorned for her husband. And I heard a loud voice from the throne saying, "See, the home of God is among mortals. He will dwell with them; they will be his peoples, and God himself will be with them; he will wipe every tear from their eyes. Death will be no more; mourning and crying and pain will be no more, for the first things have passed away." (21:1-4)

While we love the places where we live - we know we cannot "put down roots" permanently. We may love the nation to which we give our allegiance, but as citizens of heaven, we have a higher calling. Our strongest, covenanted loyalty is to the kingdom of God. It is altogether powerful and thus able to withstand all assaults against it.

Being altogether free - it is thus able to provide a perfected security for its citizens. On a particular unknown day, each one of us will have to depart this earth. On the last day of our existence here, we will be taken away from everything which we have ever known. But, in leaving this familiar country, we will be eternally blessed above in the dwelling places of heaven.

We will find that heaven is not totally "unfamiliar." Over the course of our entire lives, God has been preparing us for our departure from this earth, our journey through the vale of death, and our happy arrival in our eternal home. We will be held in a state of bliss - an existence of perpetual delight. Simply stated, we will enjoy being in "the Father's house." We will be with God and with Christ - never to be separated out, never to be left alone. Most wonderfully, also, we will be with our dear friends and loved ones who have departed this life never to be separated from them, never to be left alone.

Our going to the "mansions" above – will become a source of blessing to those who remain behind. Their sadness at our departure will be assuaged by consoling remembrances. They will recall and celebrate the fact that, above all else, we were good and faithful "pilgrims and strangers upon the earth." Their recollections of our faithful journeying will give them courage to walk strongly upon their own path of life.

Four

MOTHER OF THE FAITHFUL
Sarah

"Be Still my Soul"

Be still, my soul; the Lord is on thy side,
Bear patiently the cross of grief or pain;
Leave to Thy God to order and provide;
In every change He faithful will remain.
Be still my soul; thy best, thy heavenly Friend
though thorny ways leads to a joyful end.

Be still, my soul; thy God doth undertake
To guide the future as He has the past.
Thy hope, thy confidence, let nothing shake;
All now mysterious shall be bright at last.
Be still, my soul; the waves and winds still know
His voice who ruled them while He dwelt below.

Be still, my soul; though dearest friends depart
And all is darkened in the vale of tears;
Then shalt thou better know His love, His heart,
Who comes to soothe thy sorrows and thy fears.
Be still, my soul; thy Jesus can repay
From his own fulness all He takes away.

Be still, my soul; the hour is hastening on
When we shall be forever with the Lord,
When disappointment, grief, and fear are gone,
Sorrow forgot, love's purest joys restored.
Be still, my soul; when change and tears are past,
All safe and blessed we shall meet at last.
(Catharine Schlegel, 1752, Psalm 46:10, *The Book of Praise*. Presbyterian, Canada. 1972)

In Genesis, chapter 11, we are given an historical account of the descendants of Terah, the father of Abraham – who is known to us as the grand patriarch "Father of the Faithful" which we understand to be the people of God everywhere and for all time. Terah lived in Ur of the Chaldees on the banks of the Eurphrates river. Later on, Ur became the city of Babylon. Terah's three sons were Abram (later called Abraham), Nahor, and Haran.

We are told that Haran died before Terah, and that Abram and Nahor took wives to themselves. The name of Abram's wife was Sarai (later changed to Sarah). The root meaning of her name is "princess." We are told the ancestry of Nahor's wife, but are not given the ancestry of Sarai, which gives rise to some suspicion as to what her lineage was exactly.

Later on, in chapter 20, of Genesis, we learn that Sarah was the half sister of Abraham. She was the daughter of his father, Terah, but not the daughter of Abraham's mother. We can certainly suspect that Sarah may have been illegitimate. In any event, she did not have the highest of ancestral pedigrees. Marriage among close relations was common at that time. It was not unusual for a man to marry his half sister. In verse 30, of chapter 11, we are given some important information about Sarah's life with Abraham which was a key factor in the story of her life.

Now Sarai was barren; she had no child.

Abraham's father, Terah, journeyed from Ur of the Chaldees to an area called Haran (same name as his son). His intention was to settle eventually in the land of Canaan. Terah died in Haran – not having reached Canaan. As previously noted, Abraham then received his call from God to journey into Canaan which was to become the promised land for the people of God.

> Now the Lord said to Abram, "Go from your country and your kindred and your father's house, to a land that I will show you. I will make you a great nation; I will bless you and make your name great; and you shall be a blessing. I

will bless those who bless you; and I will curse him who curses you; and in you all the families of the earth shall be blessed." (Genesis 12:1-3)

Abraham did what God called him to do – he departed for Canaan with his wife Sarah, and Lot, his brother's son, along with all of their possessions and the people associated with his family at that time. When Abraham and his large "clan" arrived in Canaan, God told him that the land would be given to his descendants. Soon after, there was famine in the land and Abraham went down into Egypt for relief. When they were close to entering Egypt, Abraham became worried that the Egyptians would seize Sarah because she was beautiful and then kill him because he was her husband.

So, Abraham said to Sarah:

"I know well that you are a woman very beautiful in appearance; and when the Egyptians see you, they will say, "This is his wife'; then they will kill me but they will let you live. Say you are my sister, so it will go well with me because of you, and that my life will be spared on your account." (12:11-13)

As it turned out, Sarah was taken into the house of the Pharaoh of Egypt on account of her beauty and became one of the wives of the Pharaoh. Abraham was treated well on her account and prospered in Egypt as a result. But, when the Pharaoh and his house became afflicted with plagues – he confronted Abraham with the fact that he had lied about Sarah being his sister and not his wife. The Pharaoh thought that he was under judgment for marrying another man's wife. He ordered Abraham to take Sarah, his wife, and all that he had and depart from Egypt.

As we have already mentioned, Sarah was without child from Abraham. She was "barren" – that is how it was described. It was fortunate that Sarah did not become "with child" from the Pharaoh. As Sarah became older her barrenness was seen to be an obstacle to the fulfilment of the promise given to Abraham. Accordingly, Sarah persuaded Abraham to take to himself, Hagar, her handmaid, as his secondary wife. He did so, and she gave birth to Ishmael.

But afterwards, Sarah received the promise from God that she would herself bear a son. In the course of a year, she gave birth to Isaac, the child of destiny – the one in whom the covenant promise of God would be realized. It was at that point – that Sarah's name was changed from Sarai to Sarah.

> God said to Abraham, "As for Sarah your wife, you shall not call her Sarai, but Sarah shall be her name. I will bless her and moreover I will give you a son by her. I will bless her, and she shall give rise to nations; kings of peoples shall come from her." (Genesis 17:15-16)

We turn now to the New Testament – chapter 3, verse 4 of the first letter of Peter: "Rather, let your adornment be the inner self with the lasting beauty of a gentle and quiet spirit, which is very precious in God's sight."

Peter (for our purposes, the author of 1 Peter) counsels the wives to whom he is speaking to accept the authority of their husbands. He exhorts them to live lives of purity and reverence. He challenges them to adorn themselves not with outward adornments but with the inner adornment of "a gentle and quiet spirit." Peter then makes a connection to the women of ancient times: "It was in this way long ago that the holy women who hoped in God used to adorn themselves by accepting the authority of their husbands." (3:5)

Peter then bolsters his argument by citing Sarah as an example of submission to her husband – which then becomes the basis for his exhortation that the women of the Church should do likewise: "Thus Sarah obeyed Abraham and called him lord. You have become her daughters as long as you do what is good and never let fears alarm you." (3:6)

Peter understood that Sarah had called Abraham, "lord" when she was told that she would bear a son – even though she had been barren all her life and was advanced in years. Sarah laughed within herself at the thought that she and her aged husband, ten years older than her, would be able to come together and produce a child. Therefore Sarah laughed within herself, saying, "After I have grown old, shall I have pleasure, my lord being old also." (Genesis 18:12) Sarah is only "thinking" of Abraham as "her lord." Clearly, she did not directly address Abraham as "lord." But, certainly she would have thought of him in this way. It was customary for women at that time to be respectful and submissive towards their husbands. But, that does not mean they were lacking in spirit, initiative, faith, or courage. Sarah was a strong woman and not deficient in any of these virtues.

As noted above, Sarah did not have a distinguished ancestry. She gained prominence and acquired a good reputation by her faithfulness, perseverance, and adaptability. Her strength of character is clearly evidenced in the story of her life. We recall that Sarah had to endure Abraham's cowardice. She was forced to "live a lie" as his sister and not his wife, when they were actually married. Her husband Abraham, effectively disowned Sarah as his wife when they were going into Egypt.

In addition, we remember that Sarah was forced to submit herself to the Pharaoh of Egypt as his wife. She was thus "a kept women" in a foreign land - held captive in a strange, oppressive environment. Sarah managed to survive in that cruel circumstance - alone - away from her family and her people.

Sarah did not have an easy life! But, this remarkable woman of faith, courage, and perseverance was greatly blessed. Sarah was given an everlasting inheritance from God when her name was changed. In her new identity, she would "give rise to nations, kings, and peoples."

We acknowledge the fact that the great patriarch, Abraham, is "Father of the Faithful." But Sarah, his wife, is equally important, as the great matriarch of the people of God, and "Mother of the Faithful." The prophet Isaiah gave equal prominence to Abraham and Sarah when he spoke these words:

> "Listen to me, you that pursue righteousness, you that seek the Lord. Look to the rock from which you were hewn and to the quarry from which you were dug. Look to Abraham your father and to Sarah who bore you." (51:2)

The name Abram, meant "father." When Abram received the call of God, his name was changed to Abraham – meaning "ancestor of a multitude." The older name Sarai, meant "princess." Even though she was not of noble birth, Sarai's name was changed to Sarah when she received the promise that she would become "the mother of the faithful." "Sarah" was simply a newer, updated version of the older name.

The update in her life was that she would no longer bear the shame of barrenness. She would have pleasure with her aged husband and Sarah's womb would be fruitful.

Sarah's handmaid Hagar, and her son, Ishmael, had their place in the providence of God – but, the covenant line of promise, was destined to come through Sarah and Issac. The "mother of the faithful" suffered in many ways. But, women of faith everywhere can rightfully consider themselves to be the spiritual daughters of Sarah. She is truly "the spiritual mother" of all those women who are called and chosen to inherit the promises of God. This obviously applies to all the women of God – whether they bear children or not. The Sarah of old, the Sarah of Scripture, is truly a good and lasting example to all those, men and women alike, whose desire it is – to fearlessly do what is good and right and true.

With the "Mother of the Faithful" in mind, our prayers are with women the world over who are forced to submit themselves to men who have no respect whatsoever for them as women. They are enslaved in lives of misery. They are kept in oppressive, cruel situations which undermine their dignity and destroy their integrity.

We pray for their deliverance.

With the "Mother of the Faithful" in mind, our prayers are with women the world over who are forced to bear children from men for whom they have no passion and absolutely no love.

May their spirits will remain strong.

With the "Mother of the Faithful" in mind, our prayers are with women the world over who desperately hold their starving and dying children in their arms, because "engines of destruction" and "empires of oppression" run rampant in their homelands.

We pray that these horrendous sufferings will end.

With the "Mother of the Faithful" in mind, our prayers are with women the world over whose daughters are carried off by unfeeling tyrants and conscripted soldiers into slavery. They simply want their lands and their offspring to be educated in the truths of freedom, peace, and equality. It is undeniably their right.

We pray against the evil which exalts ignorance and glorifies violence.

With the "Mother of the Faithful" in mind, our prayers are with women the world over who are strong in faith, loyalty, and love, blessed as they are with a certain measure of security, protection, and good health.

May their courageous faith and example sustain them and those whom they love through difficult times of testing.

Blessed are the poor in spirit, for theirs is the kingdom of heaven.
Blessed are those who mourn, for they will be comforted.
Blessed are the meek, for they will inherit the earth.
Blessed are those who hunger and thirst for righteousness, for they will be filled.
Blessed are the merciful, for they will receive mercy.
Blessed are the pure in heart, for they will see God.
Blessed are the peacemakers, for they will be called children of God.
Blessed are those who are persecuted for righteousness sake, for theirs is the kingdom of heaven.

Matthew 5: 3-9

Five

AWESOME PLACES OF DESTINY
Jacob

We are Climbing Jacob's Ladder

We are climbing Jacob's ladder,
We are climbing Jacob's ladder,
We are climbing Jacob's ladder,
Soldiers of the cross.

Ev'ry round goes higher, higher,
Ev'ry round goes higher, higher,
Ev'ry round goes higher, higher,
Soldiers of the cross.

Brother, do you love my Jesus,
Brother, do you love my Jesus,
Brother, do you love my Jesus,
Soldiers of the cross.

If you love Him, you must serve Him,
If you love Him, you must serve Him,
If you love Him, you must serve Him,
Soldiers of the cross.

We are climbing higher, higher,
We are climbing higher, higher,
We are climbing higher, higher,
Soldiers of the cross.
(Traditional African American Spiritual)

"The stairway to heaven"

As a young boy, growing up in Victoria, British Columbia, the highlight of my summer was going to camp. For nine summers in a row, I attended the Young Mens' Christian Association (YMCA) camp at Glinz Lake, Sooke, twenty miles north and west of Victoria. Each Sunday morning at camp an outdoor church service was conducted on a high cliff overlooking the lake. It was a beautiful, natural setting with a quaint, rustic atmosphere. There we were - one hundred and twenty boys in number sitting on logs cut out to make church pews.

The church services in that setting are firmly etched in my memory as deeply meaningful and memorable. To get to the "chapel, as it was called, we had to ascend "Jacob's ladder." The "ladder" was ninety seven steps on a wooden stairway built into the side of the cliff. As we were "marched up" to the chapel, we called out the number of the steps on our way upwards. The number chorus relieved the strain of our climb up the "ladder." The Jacob's ladder of scripture has been immortalized in an African American spiritual. (see opening page of this chapter)

When I was attending "Y" Camp as it was called, I had no idea what shape or direction my life would take. I had no knowledge at that time of where I would go, what I would do, or who I would be with in my life. It was all before me - yet to be, not yet accomplished, in the destiny which would be my particular life.

As I was sitting in the outdoor chapel at "Y" camp in worship with all of the others, I remember being very aware of the presence of God.

I sensed God's Spirit over and above the rocks, trees, and hills which surrounded me. I felt God's love being communicated to me in the worship service through the readings, the prayers, and the message. It was a special, sacred, "holy" place for me.

In the Old Testament book of Genesis, chapter 28, we read about the patriarch, Jacob, as he journeyed from Beersheba to Haran. Jacob came to a certain, unnamed place and stayed there for the night. He laid his head on a stone and fell asleep. Jacob had an amazing dream that night. In the dream, there was a ladder set up on the earth which reached all the way to heaven. Angels of God were seen ascending and also descending upon the ladder.

God spoke to Jacob in the dream and gave him a wonderful blessing:

> "I am the Lord, the God of Abraham your father, and the God of Issac; the land on which you lie I will give to you and to your offspring. (vs.13) Know that I am with you and will keep you wherever you go and will bring you back to this land, for I will not leave you until I have done what I have promised you." (vs.15)

Jacob's ladder, "the stairway to heaven," was a sign from God, the sovereign Lord of heaven and earth. It was given to Jacob as a symbol of God's providential guidance being guaranteed to him for his entire life. It was a pledge of God's loving presence which would stay with Jacob all the days of his life.

In Jacob's amazing dream angels were "ascending and descending" we are told, up and down the ladder. The messengers of God were hovering - over and around, nearby and close, yet also seeming to be far away at one and the same time. The angels' mysterious presence highlighted destiny. Their awesome activity signaled transcendence.

Jacob's life was to be shaped in time and history by the Eternal One, the Creator and ruler over all that was, and is, and is to come. Jacob was greatly moved by his experience that night. He sensed the presence of the Lord in the place where he had slept. As he awoke, he cried out: "How awesome is this place! This is none other than the house of God and the gate of heaven." (vs.17). Jacob took the stone that had been his pillow, poured oil on the top of it, and called the place Bethel. He then made a vow to God that if he were sustained and protected he would be true and faithful to God.

Jacob was an amazing person of faith and resilience. He was truly a great patriarch, a father of all the faithful, in the line of descent from Abraham his grandfather, and Isaac his father. The guilt and fear which he carried in his heart was overcome by the presence of God. When he awoke he embraced the new transcendent reality represented in his dream. Jacob's undefended, vulnerable sleep in a lonely place, with an unyielding rock for a pillow became for him a place of softening and receptivity. It provided a place of entry for God's awesome, challenging presence.

We learn about destiny and transcendence from the story of Jacob and his dream. As persons of faith we believe that God's providential guidance is guaranteed to us for our entire lives. We have the hopeful assurance that God's loving presence will stay with us all the days of our lives. Our destiny is with God – the transcendent One who comes to us in mercy, love, and power. Thus and therefore, we are not alone as we journey through life. God is with us at all times and in all places. Our destiny is to live in hope, dwell in safety, inherit blessing, and then at the end – to die at peace – peace with ourselves, with life, and with God. In Psalm 139, we read these words:

> "If I take the wings of the morning and settle at the farthest limits of the sea, even there your hand shall lead me, and your right hand shall hold me fast." (vs. 9-10)

No matter where we go in life, or what we do – God is with us. If we fly away, as it were, on "the wings of the morning" to a real or an imaginary place, God is there. If we build a dwelling place in a far away distant land, God will "hold on" to us just as tightly there – as at the place of our departure. At each and every one of our Bethels, our places of destiny and transcendence, God will come to us in dreams and visions of mystery and wonder. We will receive a special blessing from "on high." Guardian angels will descend from heaven. They will hover close by to impart blessing and they will ascend upwards in order that our destiny will be confirmed forever in the vast, infinite spaces of heaven. With a rock for a pillow upon which to lay down our head, and the stairway to heaven towards which we can raise our head – our lives acquire eternal meaning and an ultimate purpose.

Here is an ancient prayer attributed to St. Columba for the travels we will make in our journeying through life:

The path I walk, Christ walks in it. May the land in which I am, be without sorrow. May the Trinity protect me whereever I stay - Father, Son, and Holy Spirit.

Bright angels walk with me - dear presence in every dealing. In every dealing, I pray that no one's poison may reach me.

May I arrive at each place. May I return home. May the way in which I spend, be a way without loss. May the path before me be smooth - man, woman, and child welcome me - a truly, good journey. Well does the fair Lord show us a course and a path.

When we look back over our lives, we often wonder how we ever made it through times of difficulty, trouble, and sorrow. Many people of faith will say that they did - with God's help and the merciful love and compassion of others given freely to them when they needed it the most. They overcame what seemed to be insurmountable. They raised themselves up out of despair. They walked proudly through adversity. They were able to hold their heads high as beloved and blessed children of God.

Verses of Psalm 46 come to mind (note the reference to Jacob): "God is our refuge and strength, a very present help in trouble. Therefore, we will not fear. The Lord of hosts is with us; the God of Jacob is our refuge." (vs. 1, 11)

When Jacob woke up in the morning at Bethel, his heart was filled with exuberance and his spirit was alive with joy. He had a positive faith inspired outlook. His awesome encounter with God gave him a truly optimistic mind set. The living God had come to him, most wondrously and convincingly in the night. Jacob could now move forward in faith, hope, and confidence.

In the daily devotional book for men, *Touchstones*, we have this meditation:

Many of us take a negative outlook. We don't believe things will work out well for us. We don't think we will have a good day. This is faith in the negative. We cannot force positive things to occur. We can only be open to them and believe in the possibility. When we expect only bad things - we squelch many good things - or, we overlook them. We must be more open and welcoming of the good things that come our way. (July 12)

As people of faith we want to direct our lives towards abundance and away from scarcity - abundance of faith, charity, and compassion. Sometimes, what we possess and experience is minimal. During those times of scarcity, we must safely guard that which remains and hold it close to our hearts. In the fullness of God's love that which is minimal is often, to our amazement, maximized into wonderful forms of abundance.

Sometimes what we possess and experience is maximal - in terms of our expectations of what is humanly desirable. During such times of defined, satisfied abundance, we must not cling too closely to that which we possess and experience. They can be encumbrances rather than blessings. In our special, awesome places of destiny - our lives, like that of Jacob's, are taken beyond that which we possess and experience into greater realms of contentment and satisfaction. As we stay fixed largely in those places, allowing them to envelop us in the minutia of our own particular lives, we discover that "walking faithfully with God" - in and through all the seasons of our lives - is indeed and in fact our true destiny.

You are holy, enthroned on the praises of Israel. In you our ancestors trusted; they trusted, and you delivered them. To you they cried, and were saved; in you they trusted, and were not put to shame. It was you who took me from the womb; you kept me safe on my mother's breast. On you I was cast from my birth, and since my mother bore me you have been my God.

Psalm 22: 3-5; 9-10

Six

MISFORTUNE REVERSED
Joseph

Balm in Gilead

Refrain
There is a balm in Gilead
To make the wounded whole,
There is a balm in Gilead
To heal the sin-sick soul.

Sometimes I feel discouraged
And think my work's in vain,
But then the Holy Spirit
Revives my soul again. (to *Refrain*)

Don't ever feel discouraged,
For Jesus in your friend;
And if you lack for knowledge,
He'll ne'er refuse to lend. (to *Refrain*)

If you cannot sing like Peter,
If you cannot preach like Paul,
You can tell the love of Jesus
And say, "He died for all." (to *Refrain*)
(Traditional African American Spiritual)

The story of Joseph in the Old Testament is a fascinating example of how something bad can be turned into something good. It was all made possible through the agony and the joy of forgiveness.

In Genesis, chapter 37, it is recorded that Joseph's father, the patriarch Jacob, loved him more than any of his other sons. "Now Jacob loved Joseph more because he was the son of his old age." (verse 3)

Parents in general and younger parents in particular do not always value and appreciate their children equally. They may tend to project their own personal ambitions and desires upon their offspring - wanting them to be exact carbon copies of themselves. This attitude and action is extremely hard on the children. Older parents have usually mellowed a certain amount and have become more tolerant and accepting of their children's uniqueness.

When children are born to an older parent they may be preferred to the ones born earlier for certain reasons. They will be regarded as precious simply because they are the last ones to be given, as it were, to the parent. There is also the contributing factor of the parent being satisfied that even in their final years they have been able to perpetuate themselves. That's exactly how it was with Jacob and his much beloved son, Joseph, "the son of his old age." Jacob had a much greater love for Joseph than his other ten sons who were born to him before Joseph. In addition, it must be noted that Joseph was the first born child of his mother, Rachel, who was Jacob's second wife, but his truest love.

Benjamin was the second born and the last child to be born to Rachel and Jacob. As a token of his affection for Joseph, Jacob presented him with a brilliant, multi coloured robe. Jacob was no doubt well intentioned.

But, his particular affection for Joseph amounted to favouritism. Jacob exalted, and, in that sense, elevated one son above all of the other eleven. We are not surprised, when we are told, in verse 4, about the way in which Joseph's brothers reacted. When Joseph's brothers saw their father loved him more, they hated Joseph and could not speak peaceably to him.

Favouritism gives rise to jealousy. It can provoke envy. If left unchecked, it can be very destructive. A dark, ominous cloud descended over Jacob's lands and his household because Jacob did not love his sons equally. His actions brought discord and hostility into their midst. All of them would suffer as a result.

A fateful drama of discord began to unfold. One night, Joseph had a dream. Somewhat unwisely, in his preoccupation with himself, he told his brothers about his dream:

> "There we were binding sheaves in the field. Suddenly my sheaf rose and stood upright. Then your sheaves gathered round and bowed down to my sheaf." (Genesis 37:7)

Joseph's brothers quickly understood the meaning of the dream. Here is their reply and their reaction:

> "Are you indeed to reign over us? Are you indeed to have dominion over us?" So they hated him even more because of his dreams and his words. (verse 8)

One day, out of sight of their father, the brothers stripped Joseph of his "coat of many colours" and threw him into a pit. A traveling caravan of Ishmaelites was passing by at that time. His brothers sold Joseph as a slave, and he was carried off to Egypt. They then took Joseph's beautiful robe and soaked it in the blood of a goat. Returning to their father Jacob, they pretended that Joseph had been devoured by a wild animal. Jacob's heart was broken. He tore his garments, put on sackcloth, and mourned the loss of his favourite son for many days refusing to be comforted.

However, for Joseph, his misfortune was soon reversed and turned into something good. The transformation of that which was seemingly bad into something incredibly good defined his entire life. There was a great providential ruling over Joseph's life which was clearly above and beyond the ordinary.

Having been sold into slavery by his brothers, Joseph found himself in the household of Potiphar, a high official in the court of the Pharoah, the king of Egypt. Here is what transpired in that circumstance:

> The Lord was with Joseph, and he became a successful man in the house of his Egyptian master, Potiphar. His master saw that the Lord caused all that he did to prosper in his hands. Joseph found favour in his sight and attended him; he made him overseer of his house and put him in charge of all that he had. (Genesis 39:2-4)

The ancient chronicler of the story highlights Joseph's "good luck" as coming to him from the providence of God. It was the determining factor and basically the underlying cause. As a consequence, there was an overflowing of blessing in and upon Joseph's life which extended to others as well. Here is how it is expressed in the narrative:

> The Lord blessed the Egyptian's house for Joseph's sake; the blessing of the Lord was on all that Potiphar had, in house and field. (verse 5)

The providential power and mercy of God lifted Joseph above the unfortunate circumstances which had changed his life so dramatically. But, his overcoming of misfortune was also due to the fact that he himself cooperated fully with the providence of God. Joseph was gifted with great intelligence and discernment. He accepted that which came upon him and made the most out of every situation. Joseph lived his life in and under God's providential ordering of circumstances - but his unique, personal "giftedness" was exercised expansively. His intelligence enabled him to quickly assess how he must act, and his powers of discernment directed him towards wise and careful responses.

Joseph had every right to be angry with his brothers for their intense jealousy and their vicious, cruel treatment towards him. Bitter feelings of anger and resentment could have entirely ruled his life. But, that was not the way of Joseph. Even though he was alone in a strange, foreign land with none of his own people to comfort him, he kept his composure and became strong within himself. Joseph prospered in Egypt even though he had begun his life there as a slave. He became a man of influence and renown because he delighted himself in God. The corresponding truth of the matter was that God took great pleasure and delight in Joseph.

In the narrative, we are told that "the Lord was with Joseph" and that he fully cooperated with God's influence and presence in his life. But, in actual fact, Joseph had every right to be angry and bitter at God for the suffering which had come upon him. He could have quite understandably blamed God for allowing such terrible things to happen. None of that seems to have taken place. Joseph kept himself close to God and God's response was to stay close to Joseph. The corollary is also true. God kept "himself" close to Joseph and Joseph responded by staying close to God. Their intimate relationship continued one event after another, one calamity after another, one challenge after another, one success after another.

Joseph lived a life of special destiny in Egypt. Eventually, he was taken into the inner circle of the ruler of all Egypt, the Pharoah. He became the Prime Minister of Egypt second only to the Pharoah in power and influence. When some years later, a severe famine arose in all of the lands surrounding Egypt, the aging Jacob sent the ten sons, who had betrayed Joseph down into Egypt to buy grain. They were obliged to appear before the Prime Minister who, as stated, was Joseph. The ten brothers did not recognize the brother whom they had treated so cruelly. When Joseph disclosed his identity to them, they bowed down before him just as it had been predicted in Joseph's dream many years before.

By way of analysis of Joseph's personality, it is clearly evident that he kept his composure in demanding, stressful situations. We can also accurately say that he made "the most of things" turning misfortune into prosperity as he rose above difficult circumstances and triumphed over events which could have easily plunged him into the depths of despair. However, the reversal of misfortune in Joseph's life cost him dearly. He paid a high price in suffering. Joseph endured the lonely agony of being completely cut off from his entire family and his beloved homeland. When he was in Egypt, there was no guarantee that he would ever see his father and mother again. Joseph did not have any assurance, whatsoever, that he would ever be able to return home.

It is not surprising, therefore, that some powerful emotions came to the surface when Joseph revealed his identity to his brothers. The book of Genesis takes us right into the heart of the dramatic event:

> Joseph could no longer control himself before all those who stood by him, and he cried out, "Send everyone away from me." So, no one stayed with him when Joseph made himself known to his brothers. He wept so loudly that the Egyptians heard it, and the household of Pharaoh heard it. And Joseph said to his brothers, "I am Joseph." (45:1-3)

In spite of his pent-up grief over being betrayed by his brothers, Joseph was able to bless them with these words:

> "Do not be distressed or angry with yourselves because you sold me here - for God sent me before you to preserve life, and to keep alive many survivors of our people. It was not you who sent me here but God." (45:5-8)

A beautiful reconciliation took place. Joseph kissed all his brothers and wept upon their shoulders. They talked with him for the first time as true brothers and true friends.

Genesis chapter 50, verses 19-21, records the words which Joseph spoke to his brothers after the death of their father, Jacob. They were worried that Joseph might still bear a grudge against them. But clearly, they had nothing to fear. Here is what Joseph said to them:

> "Do not be afraid! Even though you intended to do harm to me God intended it for good in order to preserve a numerous people. Have no fear, I myself will provide for you and your little ones."

After meeting his brothers, Joseph gave instructions that his father, Jacob, was to be brought down into Egypt. When Jacob met Joseph after being separated from him for many years, he was ecstatic. He exclaimed: "I can die now my son; having seen for myself that you are still alive." (Genesis 36:30)

When the time came for Jacob's final parting, he blessed Joseph's sons with these words:

> "The God before whom my ancestors, Abraham and Isaac walked; the God who has been my shepherd all my life to this day, bless these boys and in them let my name be perpetuated, and the name of my ancestors Abraham and Isaac; and let them grow into a multitude on the earth." (Genesis 48:16)

Joseph was given a special "coat of many colours" when he was a young boy. The coat was a sign and symbol of his remarkable life. The different colours of his coat represent the various events of his life. The many different strands are signs of the "twists and turns" of his destiny in God. The colours of his coat were woven into one fabric. Likewise, Joseph's life became seamless over time. There was a straight line of development from beginning to end. Events and circumstances unfolded as they were meant to unfold. Joseph's destiny in God was completely "fleshed out" over the days and times of his remarkable life.

It is the same with us. A beautiful tapestry is being woven from our days and times. A seamless robe is being given to us. It is a sign of our destiny in God. That which comes to us seemingly as harmful is intended for our good. Terrible circumstances may come upon us. But, God is with us - to take us through the hard times. Awful events may knock us down. God is there to lift us up. Often, sometime later, long after a troubling circumstance has occurred, we realize that it was "a blessing in disguise." Angels have been watching over us. We were rescued out of our distresses. We were lifted up out of the difficulties which threatened to destroy us. God has been the shepherd of our days. We have been blessed with favour. A good heritage will issue forth from our days. The legacy which will follow on from our lives will be an accurate reflection of the fact that we have lived with a destiny and died being truly blessed by the Lord and giver of life.

A key element in the unfolding and receiving of good things in our lives is the joy and agony of forgiveness. That is exactly what

Joseph experienced. He forgave his brothers and the reconciliation with them which followed brought him great joy. However, before this could take place, Joseph had to spend many years suffering in agony of mind and soul. It was only then that he could "let go" of his legitimate anger and outrage over what his brothers had done to him. Like Joseph's special robe, his "technicolour" coat, forgiveness has many colours. First of all, there is the red colour of rage. Something terrible happens and we are intensely angry. Our anger is often fully justified. It has, therefore, it's essential place and its own special work to accomplish. However, when we are angry we are not ready to extend forgiveness or accomplish reconciliation. Our anger must pass into a calmer place. Then and only then, will we be ready to act and respond in a good and proper way. Otherwise, we may regret our actions and responses. Reconciliation cannot take place when the red colour of rage is in full control of our hearts and minds.

Then, there is the blue colour of deep emotion. The feelings go down into our souls and spirits. We need to simply "brood" for awhile. The tears of anguish go inward. Our sadness enters into a deep lagoon of inner containment. Like Joseph, we need a time of exile, a long time far away in order for everything to settle. There is a necessity for some distance to be put between us and that which has caused us pain. We need to step away physically as well as mentally from those who have caused us grief. We may deliberately choose the time apart. Or, it may simply come upon us from outside ourselves.

Next comes the green colour of fertility. The ground of our souls is ready to allow growth and change to take place. Positive feelings of tolerance spring up. Productive actions of acceptance begin to emerge. We are no longer bitter or resentful. A "greening" time takes place. Reconciliation and a new "birthing" process are now possible. It is a season of fertile abundance. Forgiveness comes into a full flowering of beauty. Relationships blossom with fecundity. There is a delightful earthiness in our friendships. We imagine ourselves to be one with the earth, united also with everything around us which is coloured green.

There is also, the yellow colour of joy. It appears when tears of release are shed on the shoulders of those who have treated us harmfully. Joseph and his brothers stood in the place where joy overwhelmed them. They were jubilant when they met after being apart from one another for so long - ecstatic when the walls dividing them were torn down. Warmly embraced by forgiveness, they hugged one another, we could say, into a completely new life together. The yellow colour of joy was their portion. The sunshine of a new morning dawned upon them without needing any reference to the time of day.

Continuing along with the theme of forgiveness, we shall now focus our attention upon Jesus Christ - specifically, at the time of his death. When he was dying upon the cross, Christ's anguished gaze beheld those positioned below him who were his murderers. His sorrowful eyes fell upon the ones who were causing him immense suffering and untold misery. They were calloused individuals, a shameful crowd of mockers banded together in barbarism, deadened by disregard, united in a total lack of compassion by the authoritarian forces which commanded their actions and paid them their due recompense. We are told that Jesus fixed his anguished gaze upon some of them, perhaps all of them. As he lifted his aching shoulders, raised his weakened neck, angled his head heavenward, and parted his reddened lips - he put forth this prayer to his Father in heaven: "Father, forgive them; for they do not know what they are doing." (Luke 23:34)

In the final moments of his earthly life, Jesus lifted himself high above the cruel circumstances which were claiming his life. His own people had turned against him. He had been cruelly mocked and scourged by foreigners. Remembering the words of the prophet, Isaiah, we recognize that: He was despised and rejected, a man of sorrows, acquainted with grief. (53:3)

Jesus Christ was, like Joseph, an exile in a strange land. He had been sold into a form of slavery by his own kinfolk. Those of his own race and clan became his oppressors in their betrayals of him. Reversing what was his supposed misfortune, Jesus triumphed over them as the triumphant ruler of an eternal kingdom - a country without borders, wherein dwells a greatly expanded kinfolk, those of "every tribe, tongue, and nation."

47

The enemies of Jesus, those who held power in religion and state, placed burdensome chains upon him. Jesus broke loose from the fetters which bound him. Like Joseph long before him, his supposed misfortune was reversed. Jesus was at peace with himself. He thought, he believed, he was convinced that "God intended it all for good." The Father in Heaven was the shepherd of his earthly life. The tapestry of his life was being woven into one. We picture him being given, at the end, his own "coat of many colours" - a sign, a symbol of special favour and approval.

The author of the book of Hebrews in the New Testament, has put forward a remarkable assertion about Christ's attitude towards his own death. His single minded determination has been and will continue to be a profound source of inspiration for all those who wish to follow him.

> Therefore, since we are surrounded by so great a cloud of witnesses, let us lay aside every weight and the sin that clings so closely, and let us run with perseverance the race that is set before us, looking to Jesus the pioneer and perfecter of our faith, who for the sake of the joy that was set before him endured the cross, disregarding its shame, and has taken his seat at the right hand of God. (12:1-2)

In his *Letters and Papers from Prison*, Dietrich Bonheoffer gives us his own profound insight into the relationship of endured misfortune to transformed joy. Here is what he wrote:

> God allows himself to be edged out of the world and on to the Cross. God is weak and powerless in the world, and that is exactly the way, the only way, in which he can be with us and help us. It is not by his omnipotence that Christ helps us, but by his weakness and suffering. (pg. 122)

In order to "run with perseverance the race that is set before us" we must learn to forgive as Jesus Christ forgave. We will need to pray, "Father, forgive them (our oppressors and enemies) for they do not know what they are doing."

It will be necessary for us to come to the place in our hearts and minds where we do not intend any harm to come upon those who have harmed us. We will want the best for them. We will not have any wish or desire for revenge or recrimination. Where there is an opening for reconciliation we will welcome it. When a bridge can be built between us and those with whom we are estranged we will be eager to build it. When there can be some release and respite from the static situation in which we find ourselves, we will gladly embrace the opportunity for change.

In the story of Joseph we learn that God can bring good out of that which is seemingly harmful. Misfortune can be reversed. That which is extremely difficult can reap rewards as the providential will of God is accomplished in our lives. That which must be endured for a time – later on becomes a source of blessing.

In conclusion, our thoughts are pleasantly carried away into two verses, the first and second, of the beautiful hymn, *Be Still My Soul:*

> Be still, my soul: thy God doth undertake
> To guide the future, as He has the past.
> Thy hope, thy confidence, let nothing shake;
> All now mysterious, shall be bright at last.
>
> Be still my soul: the waves and winds still know
> His voice who ruled them while he dwelt below.
> Be still my soul: the Lord is on thy side
> Bear patiently the cross of grief or pain.
>
> Leave to thy God to order and provide;
> In every change, He faithful will remain.
> Be still my soul: thy best, The heavnly Friend
> Through thorny ways leads to a joyful end.[1]

---

[1] For the entire hymn, see Chapter 4.

Seven

DESCENT INTO A FOREIGN LAND
Moses – Part One

"Go Down Moses"

When Israel was in Egypt's land,
Let My people go!
Oppressed so hard they could not stand,
Let My people go

> *Refrain*
> Go down, Moses,
> Way down in Egypt's land;
> Tell old Pharaoh
> To let my people go!

No more shall they in bondage toil,
Let My people go!
Let them come out with Egypt's spoil,
Let My people go!

Oh, let us all from bondage flee,
Let My people go!
And let us all in Christ be free,
Let my people go!

You need not always weep and mourn,
Let My people go!
And wear those slav'ry chains forlorn,
Let My people go!

Your foes shall not before you stand,
Let My people go!
And you'll possess fair Canaan's land,
Let My people go!
(Traditional African American Spiritual)

"Go down Moses" is an African American spiritual. Its specific Old Testament reference is found in Exodus, chapter 7:

> Then the Lord said to Moses, "Pharaoh's heart is hardened; he refuses to let the people go. Go to Pharaoh in the morning, as he is going out to the water; stand by at the river bank to meet him, and take in your hand the staff that was turned into a snake. Say to him, The Lord, the God of the Hebrews, sent me to you to say, Let my people go, so that they may worship me in the wilderness." (vs.14-16)

In the song, it is commonly believed that Israel represents the African American slaves while Egypt and Pharaoh represent the slave owners. In geographical terms, Egypt was pictured as being below other lands. In the context of American slavery, going "down the river," meant you were being taken down the Mississippi River to the deep South where conditions were notoriously worse. Slaves who caused trouble were sold from the northern slave states into the much harsher conditions on plantations in the lower Mississippi. This left us with the expression "sold down the River" meaning to betray, deceive, cheat, or abuse in some way.

Moses was the great deliverer of the people of Israel from slavery in Egypt. He led them out of Egypt and went with them towards the Promised Land. He received the Ten Commandments from God on Mount Sinai and delivered them to the people of God. Moses is one of the greatest spiritual leaders of all time.

Moses was highly gifted. He was a warrior, mystic, statesman, law giver, deliverer, and prophet – all rolled into one. His extraordinary, special destiny was evident from the very beginning of his life. The circumstances of his birth and infancy were highly unusual and greatly auspicious.

Hundreds of years after Joseph was Prime Minister of Egypt, the Pharaoh at that time had no regard for the people of Israel, also known as Hebrews. They had multiplied greatly in numbers. The Pharaoh feared they might rise up against him, so he made them slaves. The Hebrew population continued to grow even while they were slaves. The Pharaoh's fear of the Hebrews increased commensurately with their numbers. He decreed that all male Hebrew children be put to death.

The Pharaoh's decree was carried out ruthlessly. One Hebrew mother in particular was strongly determined that her new born male child named Moses should not die. Her name was Jochebed. When Moses was born, she succeeded in hiding him for three months. When that was no longer possible, she made a tiny papyrus basket, placed her baby in it, and set him afloat on the Nile. The child's sister, Miriam, was sent to watch the basket from the banks of the river. Little Moses could have been devoured by crocodiles, drowned in a whirlpool, or swept out to sea. But, it was not to be – as he was a special child of God, a man of great destiny.

As fortune, or more accurately, providence, would have it Pharaoh's daughter was bathing in the river when the tiny basket carrying Moses floated by. She sent her maids to fetch it, and when she saw little Moses lying in the basket crying, her heart was moved with compassion. "'This is a child of one of the Hebrews!' she exclaimed." (Exodus 2:6)

Miriam, who had been watching nearby, ran to the Egyptian

princess, and immediately said: "Shall I go and find you a nurse among the Hebrew women to suckle the child for you?" (2:7)

The Princess gave her consent. Miriam quickly brought Jochebed to the scene, who was then hired by the Princess to nurse the young infant. When Moses grew older he was taken into Pharaoh's own household and given his name, which was derived from the Hebrew verb, "moseh," meaning "to pull out." As the Princess said herself: "I drew him out of the water." (2:10). The Princess treated Moses as she would her own son.

Heroic men and women are often born in the midst of great danger. Many Hebrew infants died in Pharaoh's infanticide – but, Moses survived thanks to the ingenuity and courage of his mother and sister; and the compassion of an Egyptian princess.

Great danger likewise attended the birth of Jesus Christ. While still a very young infant, he survived what is called "the slaughter of innocents." The Judean King Herod ordered that all male children under the age of two be killed. Herod was determined that the "King of the Jews," spoken of by the wise men, should not be given any chance to realize his destiny. Herod's murderous soldiers ranged through the town of Bethlehem, the birthplace of Jesus, slaughtering all of the little infant boys – to the obvious horror of their families. Joseph, the father of Jesus, was warned by an angel in a dream of the impending danger. Exercising strong parental care, he quickly bundled up his wife and baby and departed for Egypt.

Heroic persons are often born in the midst of abandonment. They are abandoned and alone when they begin their days upon this earth. In the case of Moses, his mother, Jochebed, abandoned him to the elements of nature. She cast him upon the waters of the Nile, entrusting him to the river's currents. She allowed him to float away from her in a little papyrus basket. Jochebed decided that she would not keep Moses to herself – to do so, was to place him in great jeopardy. She abandoned him to whatever destiny, fate, or more accurately providence had determined would be his lot in life.

God was certainly with Jochebed. But, there must have been a huge ache in her heart as the little basket slowly floated away from her. When destiny has a claim upon our children, we must act fearlessly on their behalf. We must let them float upon the currents of God's calling. We must let them go – downstream to their destiny, away from us without fear of the outcome.

The infant Moses drifted for some distance down the river – how far we cannot be sure. He was alone and extremely vulnerable. He sensed his abandonment and began to cry. The river's currents were kind to Moses. They took him to where he needed to go. Miriam, his sister, was God's agent on his behalf. The Princess had a tender heart.

It all turned out for the good. Little Moses was blessed by fate and guided by providence. The Pharaoh's palace became his home; the little Hebrew boy became a Prince of Egypt. Moses was drawn out of the water in order to be baptized into destiny; ordained as it were, into the status of Saviour and Deliverer of his people.

Moses was privileged to be raised amidst the wealth and luxury of the Pharaoh's palace. But, he knew who he was – he was a Hebrew, born from among slaves, a slave himself. He may have become an Egyptian by adoption, but by birth and racial origin – he was a Hebrew.

One day, as we are told, (Exodus 2:11), Moses, by then a young man, decided to visit his own people. Being slaves – they spent their days in forced labor. Moses saw an Egyptian taskmaster beating one of the Hebrew slaves. "He [Moses] looked this way and that, and seeing no one, he killed the Egyptian and hid him in the sand." (2:12)

Acting out of racial identification with one of his own, Moses displayed an instinctual compassion. He killed the slave's oppressor, an Egyptian, even though he owed his entire upbringing to them. He lashed out at the taskmaster on behalf of all his people. His action was visceral; coming, as it did, from a deep source within him – there could be no turning back. The Pharaoh's palace was not his true home. Perhaps, Moses had known for a long time that he did not belong there.

The killing was noticed. Moses had to flee into the wilderness to escape punishment. It was there that he discovered his destiny

- in the place of exile. Away from everything he had known, Moses received God's call to be the great deliverer of his people.

We have mixed reactions to the murder of the Egyptian taskmaster by Moses. We are pleased with his capacity for righteous indignation, and we greatly admire his compassion. But, his action was rash and impulsive. He was overcome with the emotion of anger. He was not in control of himself. Moses did not act in a deliberate, mature way. The murder did not accomplish anything positive at the time. But, we are impressed with Moses' obvious physical prowess and strength. The taskmaster is quickly dispatched and buried expeditiously by one man acting alone. These characteristics, as we have defined them, reappear later on in the life of Moses.

Moses ran away to escape the consequences of his actions. There was no thought in his mind, at that point, of remaining in Egypt to help his people. He was not able, or prepared, to do anything significant for his suffering countrymen. He could only think of himself, of preserving his own life - "saving his own skin." Moses was not ready to act out his destiny. It was only just beginning to be revealed to him. He was only just beginning to sense its demands. Moses did not have the maturity of personality, at that point, to do anything else. He had not acquired the strength of character which he displayed so marvellously later on.

In the New Testament book of Hebrews, chapter 11, verse 23, we read:

> By faith Moses was hidden by his parents for three months after his birth, because they saw that the child was beautiful; and they were not afraid of the king's edict.

As a tiny infant, Moses was the object of "sweet delight." He was born into a place of receptivity; a place which enveloped him in love and caring attention. He was tucked away in a safe place because his family refused to be enveloped by fear. They sensed that the little one given to them by God was a son of destiny and a child of providence. Pharaoh could rule their labours but not their hearts.

They were free in their beliefs – those who knew the "sweet delight" of unencumbered faith.

Continuing on in the same chapter in Hebrews:

> By faith Moses, when he was grown up, refused to be called a son of Pharaoh's daughter, choosing rather to share ill-treatment with the people of God than to enjoy the fleeting pleasures of sin. He considered abuse suffered for the Christ (the Messiah) to be greater wealth than the treasures of Egypt, for he was looking ahead to the reward. (vs. 24-26)

Moses killed the Egyptian taskmaster because he observed the endless toil and abject humiliation of his people. It was a quick response to a particular distressing situation. But, it came from a deep sense of identity within him. An awareness of his racial origins and his heritage of faith had been gradually asserting itself over the influence of the Egyptian palace and his foreign mother. Moses did not read out a statement renouncing his adoption. He didn't put forward a declaration denying his imparted son-ship. He simply chose, in a given moment, to delight himself with an important identification – identification with those of his own race and nation who were being terribly oppressed.

Moses gave expression to a deep delight in faith – the faith that ill treatment endured for God brings greater rewards than personal indulgences. He was not conscious of a Messiah being at his side – but, in his actions, there was certainly a prefiguration of the activity of The One, who:

> When he saw the crowds, he had compassion for them, because they were harassed, like sheep without a shepherd. (Matthew 9:36)

Eight

STANDING ON HOLY GROUND
Moses – Part Two

"Didn't Old Pharaoh Get Lost?"

The Lord said unto Moses,
"Go into Pharaoh now,
For I have hardened Pharaoh's heart,
To me he will not bow".
Then Moses and Aaron
To Pharaoh did go:
"Thus says the God of Israel –
Let my people go."

> *Refrain*
> Didn't old Pharaoh, get lost, get lost,
> Didn't old Pharaoh, get lost, get lost
> In the Red Sea,
> True believer?

Then Moses numbered Israel
Through all the land abroad,
Saying, "Children, do not murmur,
But hear the word of God."
Then Moses said to Israel
As they stood along the shore,
"Your enemies you see today,
You'll never see no more." (*Refrain*)

Then down came raging Pharoah,
That you may plainly see,
Old Pharaoh and his host
Got lost in the Red Sea.
Then men and women and children
To Moses they did flock;
They cried aloud for water
And Moses smote the rock. (*Refrain*)

And the Lord spoke to Moses
From Sinai's smoking top,
Saying, "Moses, lead the people
Till I shall bid you stop."
(Traditional African American Spiritual)

"Take off your shoes"

In the wilderness, Moses was no doubt anxious, lonely and afraid. He was probably tortured by inner voices which reproached him for his rashness and cowardly action in running away. He was going through an inner, spiritual wilderness experience, at the same time, as he was experiencing the isolation and pain of an outer, physical wilderness.

When Moses at last arrived in the land of Midian, east of Egypt, he found his way to a well. The priest of the region, Jethro, lived nearby. Moses observed Jethro's seven daughters coming to the well to draw water. They were set upon by rough shepherds who drove them away. Moses leapt to the defense of the young women, scattered the ruffians, and drew water for the young women. Once again, his capacity for righteous indignation was revealed and his sense of compassion made visible. But, this time, Moses, acted in a more mature way. He did not injure or kill any of the shepherds, and he stayed to help the young women. Once more, we see evidence of the fact that Moses was a man of prodigious physical strength and prowess. The shepherds outnumbered him but they fled in terror.

The way in which Moses acted on behalf of the daughters of Jethro shows us that he had respect for women. A man can only truly be a man, if and when, he has respect for women. Heroic masculinity is shaped and developed not just by outward acts of power but also by creative relatedness to that which is feminine within and without.

The young women were naturally pleased with Moses, and promptly took him home to meet their father, Jethro. Moses was welcomed into Jethro's household, and offered one of his daughters in marriage. Moses agreed to accept Zipporah as his wife. He then settled down with her into the comfortable life of shepherds. Moses' life in Egypt was left far behind, as he enjoyed a time of pleasantness and predictability. It was all very nice – but, if a certain momentous event had not happened, Moses would not have become the man whom we remember today.

One day, when Moses was tending his flocks of sheep, he came to the other side of a nearby mountain - Mt. Horeb, also called Sinai. He was astonished to see a very strange sight: a bush was burning, but was not being consumed by the fire. Overwhelmed by curiosity, Moses approached the fiery bush - to see what it is all about.

Curiosity can be a good thing. The desire to know, to learn - is a good quality. By being curious; by wanting to explore and make discoveries, we grow and mature and become better persons. Such was the case with Moses before the burning bush.

When Moses was standing close by the strange bush, he heard a voice call out from it: "Moses, Moses!" Moses answered, "Here I am!" The voice continued: "Come no nearer! Take off your shoes, for the place on which you stand is holy ground. I am the God of your father, the God of Abraham, the God of Isaac, and the God of Jacob." (Exodus 3:4-6)

The voice from the fire identified itself as the God of Moses' long forgotten ancestors. Abraham had heard the same voice. It called him to leave his homeland and make his journey to the land of promise. Jacob heard the same voice. It came to him in his dream of a ladder reaching up to heaven with angels ascending and descending upon it. Moses was encountering the living God, speaking out from the bush which burned but was not consumed.

Up until then, God had been known to Moses by what he had been told about God from others. God was "all wrapped up with" the history and traditions of his people. God had acted in the past. Now God was acting in the present moment - as He spoke to Moses. Now Moses will know God directly, in personal encounter - in his own individual, personal experience.

When we experience a transcendent spiritual reality - we are given an opportunity to go beyond belief into actual knowledge. Not only are we able to believe in God, we can come to know God personally in a life transforming way. The experience will probably make us somewhat uncomfortable, but it can be deeply meaningful, and it can carry us forward into our destiny, as we obediently submit ourselves to the will of God.

The ground on which Moses stood was, in fact and in truth, holy ground. It was charged with the holy presence of God. Moses hid his face. He was afraid to look. Utilizing a voice from the bush, God told Moses that he had seen the oppression of his people in Egypt. He had heard their cries. He knew their sorrows. He was acquainted with their grief – and, was now coming down to deliver them from the hand of the Egyptians and to bring them up from that land to a land flowing with milk and honey.

Moses was told he must go to the Pharaoh: "Come, I will send you to Pharaoh to bring my people, the Israelites, out of Egypt." (3:10). Moses answered: "Who am I that I should go to Pharaoh?" (3:11)

God then assured Moses that He would be with him, and when the people were brought out of Egypt they would serve God on the exact same mountain.

Moses was called to be a warrior, mystic, statesman, lawgiver, deliverer, and, a prophet – all rolled into one. He became all of those things because he encountered God in "the bush which burned, but, was not consumed." Moses was called to be a hero – to live heroically for God. The fire of God burned in the soul of Moses, and, it could not be consumed. His soul was alive with the passion of God. His soul was sustained by the flames of God's love. The soul of Moses was "lit up" with the bright glow of God's commanding presence.

When we stand in holy places – when we truly encounter the living God, we are changed. Each one of us is called to be a hero – to live heroically for God, in our age and generation. We are called by God to go to the Pharaoh's of our day, and say, "Thus says the Lord God of Israel, let my people go!"

In order to be adequately prepared for the large tasks before us, we must believe in God. But, that is not enough. We must also know God in a personal, transformative way. We must be free from any and all inner slaveries – the bondages of self-indulgence, greed, fear, and pride. It will be necessary for us to free ourselves from the inner tyrants which control our lives. It will be required of us that we be released from the demonic shackles which hold us down. We must be free Bfree in order to serve God and glorify God in everything we say and do – in the lives given to us by God.

Like Moses we may ask, "Who am I that I should go?" We don't want to give up the comfort and security which we enjoy. We don't want to venture out into unknown territory. We would rather stay just where we are at the moment. We don't want to be anything more than what we ourselves have decided we should be in life.

Other children of God are in terrible bondage. They are oppressed and ill-treated. They are perishing for want of help. Often, lamentably, we choose to leave them exactly where they are. They need help and we do not help them. They need someone to speak on their behalf and we do not want to rise up and speak on their behalf and in their defense. They are in shackles and we do not work to secure their release. They are in bondage and we make no effort to break their chains.

When Jesus Christ was beginning his ministry, he went into the synagogue in Nazareth, on the Sabbath day, and stood up to read. He read these verses from the book of the prophet, Isaiah:

> "The spirit of the Lord is upon me, because he has anointed me to preach the gospel to the poor; he has sent me to heal the broken-hearted, to proclaim liberty to the captives...and recovery of sight to the blind, to set at liberty those who are oppressed." (Luke 4: 18-19)

The place on which Jesus stood was "holy ground." He and the Father God above, had seen the oppression of the people. Their cries for deliverance had been heard. Their sorrows were well known in heaven. Jesus was told to go - to go and secure the release of the slaves from slavery - to go and deliver the bond servants from their cruel servitude - to go and liberate the victims from their suffering.

Jesus Christ said what needed to be said. He accomplished what had to be accomplished. He not only believed in God - he knew God, for, as he said himself, "I and the Father are one!"

†††††

The God we believe in comes to us, as "a burning fire" - an awesome, compelling presence. May our love for God burn brightly, at all times and in all places, with passion and desire, love and fervent devotion.

The Christ we believe in, comes to us, as "a burning fire" - an an awesome, compelling presence. May our love for Christ burn brightly, at all times and in all places, with fascination and joy, zeal and holy awe.

> "Blessed is the man who walks not in the counsel of the ungodly, nor stands in the path of sinners, nor sits in the seat of the scornful; But his delight is in the law of the Lord, and in his law he meditates day and night. He shall be like a tree planted by the rivers of water, that brings forth its fruit in its season, whose leaf also shall not wither; and whatever he does shall prosper."

Psalm 1:1-3 New King James Version

Nine

WOMEN PROTECTORS
Deborah, Lois, Eunice

BATTLE HYMN OF THE REPUBLIC

Composed in 1861, by Julia W. Howe during the Civil War in the United States. Howe was visiting a Union Army camp on the Potomac River near Washington, D.C. when she heard the soldiers singing the song "John Brown's Body[2]." She was taken up with the strong marching beat of the song and wrote the words to the "Battle Hymn" the next day. Here is her account of what happened:

> "I awoke in the morning, and as I lay waiting for dawn, the lines of the poem began to come to my mind. I said to myself, "I must get up and write these verses, lest I fall asleep and forget them.' So I sprang out of bed, found a pen, and scrawled the verses without hardly looking at the paper."

The hymn appeared in the Atlantic Monthly in 1862. It was sung at the funerals of British Prime Minister, Winston Churchill, American Senator Robert Kennedy, and American Presidents Ronald Reagan and Richard Nixon.

---

[2] John Brown was an American abolitionist who led a short lived failed insurrection to free the slaves. He was hanged in 1859.

Mine eyes have seen the glory of the coming of the
Lord;
He is trampling out the vintage where the grapes of
wrath are stored;
He hath loosed the fateful lightning of His terrible
swift sword;
His truth is marching on.

Refrain
Glory! Glory! Hallelujah! Glory! Glory! Hallelujah!
Glory! Glory! Hallelujah! His truth is marching on.

I have seen Him in the watch fires of a hundred
circling camps,
They have builded Him an altar in the evening dews
and damps;
I can read His righteous sentence in the dim and
flaring lamps;
His day is marching on. (*Refrain*)

I have read a fiery Gospel writ in burnished rows
of steel;
"As ye deal with my condemners, so with you My
grace shall deal"
Let the Hero, born of woman, crush the serpent
with His heel,
Since God is marching on. (*Refrain*)

He has sounded forth his trumpet that shall never
call retreat;
He is sifting out the hearts of men before His
judgment seat;
Oh, be swift, my soul to answer Him! Be jubilant
my feet;
Our God is marching on. (*Refrain*)

> In the beauty of the lilies Christ was born across
> the sea,
> With a glory in his bosom that transfigures you
> and me.
> As He died to make men holy, let us live[3] to make
> men free;
> While God is marching on. (*Refrain*)

> He is coming like the glory of the morning on the
> wave,
> He is wisdom to the mighty, He is honour to the
> brave.
> So the world shall be His footstool, and the soul of
> time His slave,
> Our God is marching on. (*Refrain*)

We are first initially introduced to Deborah, our first woman protector (protectress[4]), in the book of Judges, chapter 4:

> "Now Deborah, a prophetess, the wife of Lapidoth, was
> judging Israel at that time. And she would sit under the
> palm tree of Deborah between Ramah and Bethel in the
> mountains of Ephraim. And the children of Israel came
> up to her for judgment." (vs.4, 5 NKJV)

It is of great interest to us that a woman was occupying the role of a judge so early in the history of Israel. Deborah is the only woman judge mentioned in the book of Judges. In those days, disputes were brought to persons of eminence upon whom the Spirit of the Lord was believed to rest. In the tribal structure of Israel, eleven centuries before Christ, women occupied a subordinate position. But, at certain times and occasions, they did rise to positions of prominence.

Deborah's gifts must have been many and great. Seated under a

---

[3] Originally: "let us *die* to make men free."
[4] Protectress: a woman who guards or defends someone or something.

palm tree, which came to bear her name, she weighed the disputes which were brought to her, and then gave her decisions, which had the effect of law. The comment is made:

> No doubt in many issues involving domestic affairs, matters pertaining to home and family life, her counsel was far better than any man's might be. (*Interpreters*, pg.713)

Like the legendary Joan of Arc, Deborah was destined to be remembered - not for her domestic expertise, but for her role in the arena of public affairs and military exploits. Deborah was outraged by Israel's subjection to the Canaanites, the original occupants of the land which had been promised to Israel. Her people urgently needed to be delivered from the threat of Canaanite oppression. Jabin, one of the kings among the Canaanite tribes, along with his general, Sisera, had nine hundred iron chariots at their disposal. They were ready to attack the people of Israel.

Deborah's response is recorded in verses 6 and 7:

> Then she sent and called for Barak the son of Abinoam, from Kedesh in Naphtali, and said to him, "Has not the Lord God of Israel commanded, Go and deploy troops at Mt. Tabor; take with you ten thousand men, and against you I will deploy Sisera, the commander of Jabin's army, with his chariots and his multitude and I will deliver him into your hand?"

We take careful note of the fact that the summons to Barak, the army commander, came from God - through a woman, the prophetess, Deborah. The name, Barack (not exactly the same, but very similar) has not been familiar in recent years. But, it has come into prominence with Barack Obama, President of the United States, 2008-2016.

The Barak in our story was hesitant to immediately obey Deborah's summons to battle. Barak said to Deborah, "If you will go with me, then I will go; but if you will not go with me, I will not go!" (verse 8). The fact that Barak wanted Deborah to accompany him showed great respect for her ability and her courage. She agreed to go with him. But, Deborah did point out to him that he would not receive the same glory for his exploits – simply because he needed the help of a woman to win the battle. Deborah was the one who would receive credit for the victory. In the history of God's people and to this day, she is the one who is remembered – not Barak.

Sisera, the Canaanite commander, gathered together a massive army which included his iron chariots. With Sisera's army arrayed before the Israelites forces, Deborah gave the order to Barak to attack. Deborah said to Barak, "Up! For this is the day in which the Lord has delivered Sisera into your hand. Has not the Lord gone before you?" (verse 14). Barak attacked Sisera and defeated him. Sisera fled from the battlefield – and, was subsequently murdered, interestingly enough, by a woman. The final conclusion is presented in verse 23:

> God subdued Jabin, king of Canaan, in the presence of the children of Israel. And the hand of the children of Israel grew stronger and stronger until they had [completely] destroyed Jabin.

We come now to a poetic song of praise attributed to Deborah. The Song of Deborah is one of the oldest pieces of poetic composition in the Old Testament. Its vigour and vitality is recognized and praised by scholars – as indicative of being contemporary with the events it describes.

The Song of Deborah highlights the intolerable situation which the people confronted at that time. It makes mention of the heroic traditions of Israel; gives an account of the battle against Sisera and his murder; and then closes with a description of the time of peace which followed.

Here are some of the verses of The Song:

When leaders lead in Israel, (and) when the people willingly offer themselves (to the Lord), they will bless the Lord! (Judges 5:2)

Hear, O kings! Give ear, O princes! I will sing to the Lord; I will sing praises to the Lord God of Israel. (vs. 3)

In our (troubled) days, the highways were deserted. Travellers walked along the byways (for fear). Village life ceased in Israel, until I, Deborah arose - arose a mother in Israel. (vs. 6, 7)

The Lord came down for me against the mighty. (vs. 13)

They fought from the heavens; the stars from their courses fought against our enemies. (vs. 20)

Thus, let all your enemies perish, O Lord. But, let those who love him be like the sun when it come out in full strength. (vs. 31)

The entire Bible and the Old Testament in particular often portrays women fulfilling roles wherein they are very much under the domination and direction of men. However, as we allow the life and teachings of Jesus Christ to be seen as paramount over all of scripture we are able to discern a general progressive advance towards an expansive, entirely respectful, and inclusive view of women. There is a clear unmistakable movement forward which affirms the full equality of women with men. The story of Deborah represents the fact that in certain circumstances women are found to be superior to men. What is most important apart from gender is a person's spiritual life - their willingness to obey God as God directs their faith and their actions.

Deborah was "a mother for all of Israel" a true matriarch for the nation. She is honoured not just for being a wife and a mother to her children, but also as a competent judge and a deliverer of her people. She is honoured and praised to this day for her role as a "mother protector" (protectress) of the entire nation – a grand "mother-figure" to all of her people. Deborah – prophetess, judge, deliverer, "mother protector" (protectress) is an enduring example of faith in God and pride of people.

In many cultures, including our own, women have traditionally been required to occupy only a domestic role. They have not, like Deborah of old, been equal to men in the prominence given to their ability to judge civil matters. Their wisdom may have been respected, in certain ways, but they were not set apart nor called upon to adjudicate complex cases of law. They may have been expected to be intelligent and knowledgeable, but only "at home" in the domestic sphere. They were not "called to the bench" of the Supreme courts of the land. Thankfully, this is not the case today among many peoples and nations of the world.

As we examine the spiritual life of Deborah, we take note of the fact that she was sensitive to the call of God in her life. She was most attentive to – "the voice of the Lord." She sensed the presence of God with her as she devotedly gave herself to her own people. Deborah's intelligence and powers of discernment were entirely dedicated to the service of the Lord and the safety and security of her people. Deborah trusted God to give her direction and guidance – not just for herself and her family but for the entire nation. Truly, she was a "mother" for all of her people.

Deborah served her people and her nation as a wise, gifted judge, prophetess, and deliverer. She also served her people as a Mother Protector (protectress). Deborah would not allow harm to come to any of her children – those in her own household, and all those outside her family circle. Deborah's "mothering" took on the role of deliverance.

She became a commander on the battlefield in order that all of her children could live in peace and safety with one another. As her Song so aptly illustrates, everything she did was to the praise of God and for the glory of God.

To add a specifically Christian perspective to our study, we turn to the Second Epistle of Paul to Timothy, in the New Testament. In the opening chapter and verses, the Apostle Paul addresses Timothy as "a beloved son." (1:1, NKJV). Paul is obviously fond of his young protégé and greatly proud of him as well. Paul tells Timothy that he prays for him "without ceasing, night and day."(vs.3) He longs to see Timothy - that his heart may be "filled with joy."(vs.4). Then, we have this - in verse 5:

> "I call to remembrance the genuine faith that is in you, which dwelt first in your grandmother, Lois, and your mother, Eunice, and I am persuaded is in you also."

Two mothers, Lois and Eunice, are given credit for possessing an authentic spirituality. Theirs was a "matriarchal" spirituality in that it played an important, expansive role in Timothy's life. They were "Mother Protectors" (each a protectress) to him as they carefully and diligently nurtured him in the faith of Christ.

Paul reminds Timothy of his ordination to Christian ministry and service with these words: "Therefore, I remind you to stir up the gift of God which is in you through the laying on of my hands." (vs. 6)

The matriarchal, mothering role of Lois and Eunice with young Timothy equipped him to serve in the world. It is evident that they did not just keep him for themselves. They nurtured his faith in order that he could be strong in his calling to believe in Christ. In addition, they had obviously encouraged him to commit himself to missionary service under the Apostle Paul's guidance and tutelage. Finally, Paul says this to young Timothy: "God has not given us a spirit of fear, but of power and of love and of a sound mind." (vs. 7)

Deborah, the Mother Protector (protectress), was not afraid of the dangers confronting her nation and her people. She protected all of her children - in and outside the home with the power of her faith, the love that was in her heart, and the sound mind which God had given to her.

Lois and Eunice, a Christian mother and grandmother, were not afraid to witness boldly and consistently - to and with - their beloved son and grandson. They protected their offspring - in and outside the home with the power of their faith, the love that was in their hearts, and the sound minds which God had given to them. As with Deborah of old, they were in their day and time – Mother Protectors (each a protectress). These three women provide a good example for all of us to follow, women and men alike, those who have given birth to children and those who have not borne children. As people of faith, we also have a calling from God to be "spiritually minded," strong and courageous Protectors of our faith and heritage in our day and for our generation.

The concern to protect our families, peoples, and nations has always been fundamental to our humanness. Every day we make small and ordinary sacrifices to ensure the safety of those whom we love. If called upon, we do not hesitate to make large and even "ultimate sacrifices" for that which stirs our hearts' loyalty and commands our deepest affections. We are delighted and happy when those whom we love are safe. We are content when our protective actions bring peace to our lands.

††††††

The Lord is my light and my salvation; whom shall I fear? The Lord is the stronghold of my life; of whom shall I be afraid? Though an army encamp against me, my heart shall not fail.

Psalm 27:1, 3

Guard the good treasure entrusted to you, with the help of the Holy Spirit living in us.

2 Timothy 1:14

Ten

DETERMINATION
NEVER TO LEAVE
Naomi and Ruth

When the night has come
And the land is dark
And the moon is the only light we'll see
No, I won't be afraid
Oh, I won't be afraid
Just as long as you stand
Stand by me.

If the sky that we look upon
Should tumble and fall
Or the mountain should crumble to the sea
I won't cry, I won't cry
No, I won't shed a tear
Just as long as you stand
Stand by me.
(Ben E. King 1960, inspired by Psalm 46:1, 2)

"God is our refuge and strength, a very present help in trouble. Therefore we will not fear, though the earth should change, though the mountains shake in the heart of the sea; though its waters roar and foam, though the mountains tremble with its tumult."

> Now it came to pass in the days when the judges
> ruled that there was a famine in the land. And a
> certain man of Bethlehem Judah, went to dwell
> in the country of Moab, he and his wife and his
> two sons. (Ruth 1: 1, NKJV)

So it is that the book of Ruth in the Old Testament begins to unfold
the story of a particular Israelite family in ancient times. A time of
great hunger had fallen upon the land of Judah. Elimelech took his
family into the nearby land of Moab. His wife's name was Naomi,
which means "lovely, delightful." The names of his two sons were
Mahlon and Chilion. Mahlon means "to be weak." He must have
been a sickly child. Chilion means "one failing or pining away."
Elimelech's name meant "God is King." Names in ancient times often
reflected profound spiritual realities.

We do not know how long Elimelech's family was in the land of
Moab. All we know is that at some point later in the story, Elimelech
suddenly died. His two sons married Moabite women, one named
Orpah, and the other named Ruth. The name, Orpah, is from the
Hebrew word meaning "neck." It meant something like "firmness or
stiff-necked." This does not imply a lack of beauty. A woman with an
impressive neck was considered attractive in those days. The name,
Ruth, signifies "friendship." This was certainly descriptive of Ruth,
as we shall discover.

The two sons of Elimelech and Naomi lived with their Moabite
wives for ten years, and then, suddenly both of the sons died. With
this tragic turn of events, Naomi lost her husband and both of her
children. She thus felt completely alone. Naomi had no further
reason, therefore, to stay in Moab. The lengthy famine in Judah was
finally over. She could return home if she wished. For, as she was
told: "The Lord had visited his people by giving them bread." (1:6)

Naomi spoke to her two daughters-in- law, Orpah and Ruth. She
told them that they must return to their own families. In this way,
they could marry again and bear children. Naomi was a woman
of great faith. In spite of her troubles, she believed strongly in the

goodness of God. She extended a "heart-felt" blessing to Orpah and Ruth with these words: "May the Lord deal kindly with you, as you have dealt with those in our family who have died and with me." (1:8)

It was a highly emotional time for the three women. We are told: "Naomi kissed them, and they lifted up their voices and wept." (1:9). Orpah suggested that they should return with Naomi to Judah. But, Naomi objected strongly. She told them that she was too old to bear any more sons whom they could eventually marry. And, even if she did, it would be too long for the younger women to wait. Being Moabites, the two women would be less likely to remarry in Judah. What else could they do there other than share Naomi's poverty and sorrow?

Naomi's concluding words were greatly sad and mournful on account of her deep love for her daughters-in-law. "No, my daughters; for it grieves me very much for your sakes that the hand of the Lord has gone out against me." (1:13)

Each one of the three women had lost a husband. Naomi had also lost her only children, her two sons. She had no grandchildren to be with either. The young widows could easily remarry if they returned to their homeland. They had every prospect of security and happiness. Naomi was willing to accept her fateful lot in life. She would live out the rest of her life as a lonely widow. For her, it was the will of God - nothing happens by chance. God is sovereign. What comes to pass has to be from the hand of God working in and through every-day circumstances and occurrences.

Naomi's woeful words provoked even more tears. Orpah kissed her mother-in-law as she said farewell. She was going to return to Moab. She wanted to be a wife once again. Ruth was not so easily persuaded. We are told that she "clung to Naomi." Ruth had given her covenanted loyalty to Naomi and her family. She was not going to leave, and thereby break away from her commitment. First and foremost, she wanted to continue on being Naomi's daughter-in-law. It was more important to her, at that decisive moment and time, to stay with Naomi than it was to secure her future as a wife and a mother in Moab.

Then, Ruth spoke these beautiful, immortalized words:

> "Entreat me not to leave Thee, or to return from following after Thee: for whither thou goest, I will go; and where thou lodgest, I will lodge. Thy people shall be my people, and thy God my God. (1:16, KJV)

> Where you die, I will die, and there will I be buried. The Lord do so to me, and more also, if anything but death parts you and me." (1:17, NKJV)

In those days, in the faith of the Lord's chosen ones – God, land, and people were one. Ruth had come to believe in the God of Israel, which was Naomi's God. She was no longer attached to the gods worshiped in Moab by her own people. Ruth had never been to Naomi's home country except through the stories Naomi had shared with her about Judah. She was willing to go there with Naomi as an act of genuine love and devotion. Her identification with Naomi was full and complete. Ruth wanted to be buried in Naomi's homeland. Her pledge was one of undying faithfulness. Her commitment was for life without any reservation or qualification. Ruth's covenantal promise was absolute – not to be revoked and without hesitation of any kind. Ruth refused to abandon Naomi. Her words were explicit and deeply heartfelt, "Entreat me not to leave Thee!"

Naomi finally accepted Ruth's determination to stay with her: "When Naomi saw that Ruth was determined to go with her, she stopped speaking to her, and the two of them went on until they came to Bethlehem." (1:18)

Ruth had resolved firmly in her mind that she did not want to leave Naomi. She fully accepted the faith of Naomi, her nation, and her people.

It was an unshakeable firmness of will – a strong commitment which gathered together everything which she was as a person. Ruth's pledge to her mother-in-law, Naomi, included an oath to God. The New English Bible translation brings this out most notably:

"Your people shall be my people, and your God my God. Where you die, I will die, and there I will be buried. I swear a solemn oath before the Lord your God: nothing but death shall divide us." (1:16, 17)

When the two widowed women arrived in Bethlehem, they had to immediately devise some way of looking after themselves. One such way was provided in the custom of gleaning. At harvest time the borders of the fields were left untouched for the benefit of the poor. They could go into the fields after the reapers and pick up anything that was left. Ruth set out one day to glean what she could from the fields of a kinsman, named Boaz. As it turned out, he was a solid citizen, a man of influence, integrity, and strong faith. Boaz had heard of Ruth's kindness to Naomi. He made sure that Ruth could do her gleaning safe and unmolested.

Ruth, we are told, fell prostrate before him, as she asked: "Why are you so kind as to take notice of me when I am only a foreigner?" (2:10, NEB)

Boaz replied: "They have told me all that you have done...you left the land of your birth, and came to a people you did not know before. May the Lord reward your deed; may the God of Israel, under whose wings you have come to take refuge, give you all that you deserve." (2:11,12, NEB)

These were not just random events which had taken place. God had been watching over everything which had transpired. Ruth and Naomi had been traveling under divine guidance and protection. Boaz recognized this as he spoke of "the wings of God," an image of hovering mercy and tender love. Everything which had taken place was in accordance with the will of the sovereign Lord God of Israel. Boaz was speaking for God when he said that Ruth was worthy of reward and blessing.

At the end of the day, Naomi pronounced a blessing on Boaz: "Blessings on him from the Lord. The Lord has kept faith with the living and the dead." (2:20, NEB)

The kindness shown by God to Ruth and Naomi was a kindness

to their dead husbands and other deceased relatives as well as to them.

As the story further unfolds, Boaz and Ruth were eventually married. Ruth conceived and gave birth to a son, named Obed. He became the father of Jesse, who was the father of David, the greatest king in the history of the nation of Israel. It was from the line and lineage of king David that Jesus Christ was born.

The love of Ruth for Naomi, her mother-in-law, is the center piece of their entire story. It received its final tribute at the end from the women who knew them as they spoke these words to Naomi:

> "Blessed be the Lord, today, for he has not left you without a next of kin...The child will give you new life and cherish you in your old age; for the daughter-in-law who loves you, who has proved better to you than seven sons, has borne him." (4:14-16, NEB)

We are reminded of a young woman spoken of in the New Testament who also displayed strong resolve in her determination to act out the will of God. Mary, the mother of Jesus, called herself "the handmaid of God" as she freely and humbly accepted the will of God for her life. The angel, Gabriel, came to her with the announcement that she would bear "the Son of the Most High" in her womb. (Luke 1:32) Mary submitted herself fully and completely to "the new land of the gospel" (remembering Ruth's willingness to accompany Naomi back to Judah) which was being "opened up" by the coming of the Christ child.

Here is the reply which Mary gave to the angel: "Let it be according to your word." (1:38 NKJV)

Mary knew that she was greatly favoured and wonderfully blessed to be thus identified with God and her own people. Her words could easily have echoed Ruth's: (paraphrased)

> "I will not return from following after Thee.
> Where I am to go, dear God, I will go.
> Where I am meant to lodge, I will lodge.

The people of God are my people.
You, O God, are my sovereign Lord.
Let it be! Let it be - to me and more also!"

God, land, and people are thus and therefore One. The people of God are united as One - One with God, One with the land they dwell upon, and One with one another.

"Thy God shall be my God!"

It is good when we can share our faith with others - especially those most dear to us. It is a source of strength and comfort to believe in the same God together. In 1 Peter, chapter 1, verse 7, faith is referred to as, "more precious than gold." In 2 Peter, it is extolled and highlighted with these opening words of the epistle:

> "To those who have received a faith as precious as ours through the righteousness of our God and Saviour Jesus Christ - May grace and peace be yours in abundance in the knowledge of God and of Jesus our Lord." (1:1,2)

As the old hymn, *Blest be the Tie*, expresses it:

> "Blest be the tie that binds,
> Our hearts in Christian love.
> The fellowship of kindred minds
> Is like to that above.
> Before our Father's throne,
> We pour our ardent prayers.
> Our fears, our hopes, our aims are one,
> Our comforts and our cares."

God, land, and people are One - "Thy people shall be my people!"

As we live out our lives in various places, we are always in some form of community with others. We are never entirely isolated from other people, and are thereby bound together by common social, cultural and religious values. We are not alone – we are very much "with" one another. We share life "from the cradle to the grave" in all of its "multi-faceted" shapes, forms, and expressions.

We build institutions together, we educate our young, we care for the sick among us, we protect one another from harm and danger. We laugh and play in the same places. We watch one another grow old. And, hopefully, we will respectfully "mark" one another's passing when we die.

The story of Naomi and Ruth is a "heart-warming" tale about two ordinary people "facing up to" trouble and sorrow together – a delightful chronicle about love as it is expressed in the bonds of friendship. Two separate persons – loved ones, those in the same family, became friends as they walked through life together sharing its joys and sorrows in company with one another. They were determined to stay together "no matter what, come what may." The love of God was strongly in evidence as the most important unifying and strengthening factor in their determination to never leave one another.

True friends, in and out of family groupings and loyalties, are loyal to one another. They are together "for the long haul," as we say. No one is leaving. No one is opting out. A true friend can be trusted to stay with you to the absolute final end, however and whenever that comes. A true friend can always be "counted on" – to be true – absolutely, without worry or hesitation. Good and true friends are reliable and trustworthy. They give us strength, confidence, and comfort as we make our journey through life together.

Even if good friends are parted for a period of time, they still keep in touch. Our best and truest friends will be "there for us" as we say, when we need them. There is no doubt in our minds A good friend "sticks up for us" when others put us down. When we are in the company of a close friend – we relax. We are perfectly and completely at ease with them. We can be ourselves. We don't have to impress them or worry about everything which we say. We know that if there are problems or tensions between us they will be dealt with – because we would never allow anything to destroy our friendship.

John O'Donohue has written the following about friendship in his book, *To Bless the Space Between Us:*

> May you be blessed with good friends.
> And learn to be a good friend to yourself,
> Journeying to that place in your soul where
> There is love, warmth, and feeling.
> May it transfigure - what is negative, distant,
> Or cold within your heart.
> May you treasure your friends.
> May you be good to them, and be there for them

Eleven

NO WRONG DOING FOR GOD
Job

Nobody Knows the Trouble I See

Refrain
Nobody knows the trouble I see, Lord,
Nobody knows but Jesus;
Nobody knows the trouble I see,
Glory, hallelujah!

Sometimes I'm up, sometimes I'm down;
O yes, Lord!
Sometimes I'm almost on the ground.
O yes, Lord! (to *Refrain*)

Although you see me going 'long so,
O yes, Lord!
I have my troubles here below.
O yes, Lord! (to *Refrain*)

One day I was walking along,
O yes, Lord!
The element opened and the love came down.
O yes, Lord! (to *Refrain*)

I shall never forget that day,
O yes, Lord!
When Jesus washed my sins away.
O yes, Lord! (to *Refrain*)
(Traditional African American Spiritual)

> There was once a man in the land of Uz whose name was Job. That man was blameless and upright one who feared God and turned away from evil.
>
> There was no better man than Job. He was kind and devout, righteous and true. Job followed the ways of God. He kept the laws and traditions. He was without equal as the "greatest of all the people of the east." (Job 1:3)

We are told that Job had seven thousand sheep, three thousand camels, five hundred yoke of oxen, five hundred female donkeys, and very many servants. The patriarch Job, was "the greatest" in terms of prosperity and material success. In those days, in that ancient agricultural society, prosperity was measured in numbers of sheep, camels, oxen, donkeys and servants. In our day, prosperity is measured in numbers of dollars, square footage of the home, the size of land possessed, and the "grandness" of one's car, truck, boat, or recreational vehicle.

Job was "greatest of all" in terms of prosperity. But, he was also the greatest with reference to personality. He was fine and noble - truly a genuinely good, virtuous, outstanding man.

The book of Job has as its theme the relationship of prosperity to goodness. A fundamental question arises, "Was Job good because he was prosperous?" We can put the question this way, "Is it easier to be good if we are wealthy?"

Referring to religion:

> "Is it easier to walk the straight and narrow path of faith in God if we have money in our pockets? Do those who have a lot of this world's goods find it easier to be blameless and upright? Is it easier to travel along through life on a highway of righteousness when things are going well?"

The story of Job in the Old Testament opens with the imaginative portrayal of a great conference taking place in the heavens concerning Job. The power of evil personified in Satan, the Devil, appears before God. The Evil One challenges the connection between goodness and prosperity in the life of Job. God's adversary and Job's enemy puts forward this bitter provocation:

> "Does Job fear God for nothing? Have you not put a fence around him and his house and all that he has, on every side? You have blessed the work of his hands, and his possessions have increased in the land. But, stretch out your hand now, and touch all that he has, and he will curse you to your face." (1: 9-11)

In modern colloquial terms, we can rephrase the Devil's words this way, "Listen God, people don't follow you for nothing! They follow you because of what they can get out of it. They're in it for the rewards and prosperity which you give them in money, vehicles, houses, property, vacation homes, and extended holidays."

Returning to our study – we note that Satan tells God that Job's language of devotion can easily give way to the language of blasphemy. The Devil challenges God to take away everything which Job has been given. Satan insists that Job's blessing of God will quickly give way to cursing. As we follow the story, we are amazed that God consents to the Devil's bitter provocation. "Very well, all that Job has is in your power; only do not stretch your hand against him (to slay him)." (1:12)

Reading on in the ancient story, we learn that a band of marauders suddenly fell upon Job's flocks of oxen and donkeys and carried them off. The servants with the animals were killed. In addition, Job was told that "the fire of God from heaven" (a bolt of lightning) had burned up his sheep and the shepherds with them. Then, he was told that his camel herd had been raided and their keepers killed. Even more calamitous, Job was informed that a mighty hurricane wind had crushed the house in which his sons and daughters were feasting and they were all dead.

Job was in great grief and deep sorrow. All of his prosperity and success was gone. He was no longer "the greatest of all the people of the east" in goods, prosperity, and possessions. He had lost all of his dear children as well.

Questions immediately follow: "Would Job continue to be blameless and upright? Would he still fear God? Would he keep walking along on the path of righteousness? Here is how Job reacted:

> Then Job arose, tore his robe, shaved his head, and fell on the-ground and worshiped. He said, "Naked I came from my mother's womb and naked shall I return there. The Lord gave and the Lord has taken away; blessed be the name of the Lord." (1:20-22)

Job's speech patterns did not change. His language was the same. He still blessed God. There was no cursing or blasphemy of any kind upon his lips. Job was still intensely devout. With nothing in his hands, he still feared and revered God – even though it was God who had supposedly allowed him to be plunged suddenly into horrible grief, sorrow, and loss.

When raging fires from arid hillsides sweep down upon homes and lives below – will those who survive bless God or curse God? Mammoth fires consume large tracts of boreal forests laying waste the land – will those who flee their homes and their towns speak the language of praise?

Sleeping on the floor in school gymnasiums with nothing left but what they could take with them in the last few minutes – will they blame God or the Devil for the calamity which has fallen upon them? Returning to their homes to see nothing but rubble, ashes, and utter devastation, all personal things gone, never to be replaced – will it be suggested to them that a capricious, fateful power has usurped the role of a beneficent providence? Did a mysterious conference in the heavens rule against them as a conflagration of flames and fire was given over to a malevolent power?

Huge, terrifying Tsunamis strike the coast lands of low lying areas. Thousands of people are killed. Thousands more lose everything they own. Their entire way of life is destroyed – their livelihoods taken from them, often never to be replaced. As with Job, they bear a double grief – the loss of precious loved ones and friends, and the loss of homes and possessions. Will they be tempted to curse the powers which rule the seas?

Returning to our story – Job is no longer a great man dwelling happily and successfully upon the hillsides of Uz. Instead, we find a pitiful, dejected, crumpled man sitting upon a heap of ashes. Satan had appeared before God, a second time. The Lord pointed out the fact that Job had held on to his integrity. Satan asked permission to "touch the bone and flesh" of Job predicting that, as a result, Job would "curse God to his face." With "loathsome sores" over his entire body, sitting upon a heap of ashes, Job was expected to revile against God for the misery he was suffering. His wife told him that he should "curse God and die."

Job would have none of it! Here is his reply: "Shall we receive good at the hand of God, and not receive the bad? (2:10). Job was brought extremely low, but he did not angrily lash out against God or charge the Almighty with malicious intent. We are told that "Job did not sin or charge God with wrongdoing." (1:22) He kept some room in his heart for devotion. There was still some praise upon his lips and some hope in his soul.

From this ancient chronicle of righteousness being sorely tested by adversity and faithfulness being challenged by despair – come these questions: Why do we in our day and generation worship God? Is it because we think we will be substantially rewarded? Why do we seek to walk in the ways of God on our journey through life? Is it because we believe we will be hugely successful?

When adversity comes to us and calamities of many different kinds fall upon us, we may conjure up the image of a conference in the heavens wherein alien forces have presented a case against us. We may begin to think that our doom has been secured, the die has been cast, the sentence has been pronounced – we are false and unworthy, pitifully weak and miserable, shallow and sinful. We must expect to be cast off, we deserve to die with nothing in our hands, hearts, or minds.

It is often characteristic of our humanness that we know how to speak to God when things are going well. We give thanks quickly, we recite prayers with ease, we fall down upon our knees without hesitation when life has favoured us with prosperity.

When we are blessed with abundance, we don't have "a care in the world." We desire wealth thinking that it will never corrupt us. We cling to the notion that we will always be good people. We vainly imagine that money, the root of all evil, cannot ever take over our hearts, minds, and souls. We foolishly think that it will never destroy us from within.

We assume that it is always good to desire wealth and pleasure, ease and security. If there are associated dangers, we think that we will somehow be protected. We consider ourselves to be invincible. We tell one another that we will "defy the odds." If trouble comes, if anything is taken away – we remain defiant. We are determined to never surrender to the truth that we have been foolish and wrong-headed, stubborn, and proud without cause.

Gustavo Gutierrez, a Latin American theologian, gives us these insights concerning the story of Job:

> The central question of the book of Job is raised at the outset: the role that reward plays in faith in God. The author is telling us that a utilitarian religion lacks depth and authenticity. It has something satanic about it. The expectation of rewards spoils the relationship with God and is an obstacle on the way to God. In self-seeking religion there is no true encounter with God but rather the construction of an idol. (Gutierrez, *Job*, pg. 3)

We have, in our flawed humanness, an innate tendency to receive as truth certain false and harmful myths which are regularly presented to us. We are predisposed to believe that we can be easily transported out of our daily drudgery into the wonderful worlds of fortune and success, fame and happiness by something as simple as a lottery ticket.

Just one example – reality shows are popular on television. But, in actual fact, they portray little or nothing of the reality which you and I must deal with each day. What they present is "un-reality." None of it would take place if it were not for the promise of money and the seductive lure of instant fame and abundant fortune. If it weren't for "the pot of gold at the end of the rainbow" the competitors would not compete, nor would the participants show up, or the hosts be given employment.

Again, in our flawed humanness, exuberant expressions of "thanksgiving" flow from long lists when we are pleased with everything we have received. We give glowing testimonies in praise of God when we think the Almighty is on our side. If we have money in our hands and an ample bank account, we don't find it hard to speak the language of praise. We say, with great gusto and deep emotion, "The Lord has given great and wonderful things to me. Blessed be, blessed be the name of my Lord" (emphasis on "me" and "my"). We easily convince ourselves that we deserve to be blessed in abundant, material ways. As our entitlement, it is purely and simply what is due to us.

Looking once again at pitiful, dejected Job, humbled by horrible calamities, brought low by cruel circumstances – "What does he say? How does he speak? What is in his heart, mind, and soul?" Here, once again, is what he says:

> "Naked I came from my mother's womb, and naked I shall return there; the Lord gave, and the Lord has taken away; blessed be the Name of the Lord." (1: 21)

Job speaks the language of praise even when things are going miserably. The old patriarch has nothing left but the ragged shirt on his back. His "millions" which is his abundance is gone. His dreams have been shattered. A cruel reality coming down from a seemingly merciless heaven has destroyed him within an inch of his life. It is, we could say, using a modern expression, a totally "un-real" experience. At one time in his life, Job was rewarded for everything he did. He worked hard and there was fruit from his labor. He was kind and good and there were direct benefits. He believed in God and everything went well. At that time in his life, there seemed to be a tight connection between faith and rewards, goodness and blessing, righteousness and prosperity. The grace and favour of God was expressed to Job in the giving of the many gifts which he received from God.

Isn't that the way we expect it to be? We work hard, and therefore, expect to be successful. We are kind and generous to others, and thus expect the winds of fortune to blow gently upon us. We believe in God and expect to find true happiness in God and from God.

With Job as our example, clearly the most difficult aspect of faith and belief is to find God's grace and favour in the taking away of gifts.

To illustrate:

We have the gift of a loved one and that most precious person dies. Can we accept it? Will we find God's grace to be sufficient through our devastating loss?

We have the gift of a job, a career, a livelihood. Suddenly it is all taken away. Can we accept it? Will we discover that God's blessing is there even in the midst of what seems to be a curse?

Can we say - will we ever be able to say, when a wonderful gift is taken away and the clouds open up with the "fires of hell" raining down upon us - those powerful, piercing words which Job spoke:

> "The Lord gives, the Lord takes away. Blessed be the Name of the Lord?"

At one point in his ministry, Jesus Christ spoke to his disciples about his imminent departure. He told them that, upon his leaving, he would ask the Father in heaven to send them another "Comforter." The "Comforter" would be the Holy Spirit who would be with them forever. The Spirit would "abide" with them and they would not be "orphaned" by Christ's physical absence. In effect, The Father, Son, and Holy Spirit would come to them in a unity of love – and, with an ongoing, abiding presence. (John 14:15-20). John chapter 14, verse 23, records these words of Jesus:

> "Those who love me will keep my word and my Father will love them and we will come to them and make our home with them."

When terrible losses come upon us we feel "orphaned" whether or not that is the actual case. We have lost that which has parented us. We no longer have any motherly nurture in our lives to console us. Gone is the fatherly guidance which we leaned upon. When awful calamities come upon us which disrupt our lives, destroy our ease, and take away our security, there is no safe physical or emotional place to return to – and no home (whether actual or not) to call our own anymore.

John 14, also records these words of Jesus:

> "Peace I leave with you; my peace I give unto you. I do not give to you as the world gives. Do not let your hearts be troubled, and do not let them be afraid." (14:27)

Hopefully, by God's grace and with the help of the Holy Spirit, we will be able to enter into the time and stand in the place where – with reference to our suffering and our losses, we will be able to say, "The Lord gives, the Lord takes away, blessed be the name of the Lord." But, as it is a work of grace and an action of the Spirit – we must not force the resolution or pre-empt the process of acceptance. It must come in its own way – according to its own timetable.

As Jesus Christ approached the end of his days among us, after many hardships and privations, trials and temptations, with death at his doorstep, he came to his own understanding and acceptance of his divine destiny. In the garden of Gethsemane, just before his arrest, trial, and condemnation:

> .... he withdrew from them (his closest disciples) about a stone's throw, knelt down and prayed, "Father, if you are willing, remove this cup (of suffering) from me; yet, not my will but yours be done." Then an angel from heaven appeared to him and gave him strength. (Luke 22: 41-43)

Twelve

A SUMMONS TO LOVE
Song of Songs

In the Bleak Midwinter
In the bleak midwinter, frosty wind made moan,
Earth stood hard as iron, water like a stone;
Snow had fallen, snow on snow, snow on snow,
In the bleak midwinter, long ago.

Our God, Heaven cannot hold Him, nor earth
sustain;
Heaven and earth shall flee away when he comes
to reign,
In the bleak midwinter a stable sufficed
The Lord God Almighty, Jesus Christ.

Enough for Him, whom cherubim, worship night
and day,
Breastful of milk, and a mangerful of hay;
Enough for Him, whom angels fall before,
The ox and ass and camel which adore.

Angels and archangels may have gathered there,
Cherubim and seraphim thronged the air;
But his mother only, in her maiden bliss,
Worshipped the beloved with a kiss.

What can I give Him, poor as I am?
If I were a shepherd, I would bring a lamb;
If I were a Wise Man, I would do my part;
Yet what can I give Him: give my heart.
(Traditional Christmas Carol)

> My beloved speaks and says to me: "Arise my love my fair one, and come away; for now the winter is past, the rain is over and gone. The flowers appear on the earth; the time of singing has come, and the voice of the turtledove is heard in our land. The fig tree put forth its figs, and the vines are in blossom; they give forth fragrance. Arise my love, my fair one, and come away." (Song 2:10-13)

One of the most fascinating books in the Bible is the Old Testament book "The Song of Solomon," also called, "The Song of Songs." Being designated as "Solomon's" can mean either that he is the author or that he is the patron. It is most likely King Solomon was chosen by the actual author (or authors) as an important personage whom he wanted to honour by referencing him as the patron of the book. Certain portions of the book may have been written in Solomon's day but most of it has its origins in a later date and time.

The Song is a marvellous addition to Holy Scripture. It is lyrical and joyous as it affirms a deeply emotional, sensual enjoyment of life, love, and the created order. It is entirely consistent with these words from the book of Ecclesiastes, likewise attributed to Solomon:

> "This is what I have seen to be good: it is fitting to eat and drink and find enjoyment in all the toil with which one toils under the sun the few days of the life God gives us. God keeps [us] occupied with the joy of [our] hearts." (5:18, 20)

Traditionally, The Song has been interpreted in an allegorical way. As an allegory, the meaning and purpose of the book is not as it appears on the surface. It is not really about human love being celebrated and enjoyed amidst the beauties and wonders of nature. As an allegory, The Song is interpreted solely in terms of the covenanted relationship of God with his people. This so called "elevation" of the book helped to secure a place for it in the canon of Scripture. To read The Song allegorically was quite natural in some ways. The fact that in the days of the New Testament this practice was standard procedure shows that it began very early. However, it is highly unlikely that The Song was meant to be read in this way. It does not need to be elevated – it clearly has a legitimate place in Holy Scripture on its own merit simply as a poem celebrating human love amidst the beauty and wonder of the created order. Recently, in modern times, the natural solely "human" interpretation of The Song, has, thankfully, gained the ascendancy.

The Song is, therefore, without apology of any kind – a straight forward, happy, and joyous celebration of human love. It is basically a collection of various wedding songs brought together in one single compilation. God is not mentioned in the Song. Common theological things like sin and salvation, duty and death are not dealt with at all.

The Song expresses itself spontaneously as it responds to the evocative prompting of love and the created order. J. C. Rylaardsdam gives us this comment:

> "The Song responds to all the stimuli of nature and, in particular, it puts into words the reactions produced by the aroused impulses of desire. It is a sensate and sensuous book in every respect." (Laymans Bible Commentary, pg. 139)

In chapter 2, verse 8 (and following), there is what is called a Springtime Rhapsody:

> My beloved speaks and says to me: "Arise, my love, my fair one, and come away; for now the winter is past, the rain is over and gone. The flowers appear on the earth; the time of singing has come, and the voice of the turtledove is heard in our land."

The bride hears the voice of the bridegroom. He is a happy herald of the coming of spring. He peeps in at the lattice of his beloved's house and tells her the good news: sunshine, flowers, the fragrance of orchards, the cooing of birds abound. Nature is alive again. He wants her to come away with him – the time is ripe for love. Great delights are in store for them.

Verses 16 and 17 provide a beautiful description of the bride and bridegroom's inspirational intimacies:

> My beloved is mine and I am his; he pastures his flock among the lilies. Until the day breathes and the shadows flee, turn, my beloved, be like a gazelle or a young stag on the cleft mountains.

The bride and bridegroom are alone for the night. They can share their deepest intimacies. They can gently and sweetly delight themselves in and with one another. The bridegroom gives pleasure to the bride as he figuratively "pastures his flock among the lilies." Like a shepherd guiding his flock towards pleasant pastures, the lover delicately directs his lovemaking desires and prowess over and among, what could be called, the flowers of femininity. Simply together, the couple enjoy one another's charms and strengths.

The bride invites the bridegroom to "turn" – and, be everything he wishes to be in masculine impulse and male excitement. She invites him to gallop like a gazelle and rise up like a young stag, as they are pictured gleefully rushing up and down a mountain divide. The youthful ardour and eagerness of the bridegroom has been described earlier on: "Look, he comes, leaping upon the mountains, bounding over the hills." (2:8)

The bride wants her strong, eager lover to be completely happy and satisfied. It is deeply sensual for the two of them, but, also deeply soulful. The bride gives us this beautiful summary: "Upon my bed at night, I sought him whom my soul loves." (3:1)

In a wedding ceremony opening statement, we have these words: "The union of man and woman in heart, body, and mind is intended for their mutual comfort and help, that they may know each other with delight and tenderness in acts of love." (Source unknown)

A man and woman in love may find themselves born to the

sweet delights of an incredibly deep communion. As they seek the one "whom their soul loves," they take themselves out beyond the boundaries of their own person, ego, and narcissistic preoccupations. An entirely new world opens up to them - with each tender expression and each kindly sensitive gesture. The layer of dark clouds above is removed. A sublime glory beckons. A heavenly calling is heard - the call to love and be lost in love. So, it is that we rise up to love even when we know the way of love is fraught with danger. We aspire to love and in the process we make ourselves vulnerable. But, there is no higher road upon which we can walk. We must make the choice to love - otherwise we will have lived in vain.

The Apostle Paul gives us his insightful reflections on love, in what is called his "hymn of love":

> "If I speak in the tongues of men and of angels, but do not have love, I am a noisy gong or a clanging cymbal. And, if I have prophetic powers, and understand all mysteries and all knowledge, and I have all faith, so as to remove mountains, but have not love, I am nothing." (1 Corinthians 13: 1, 2)

The eloquence of men and women without love is the futile sound of "nothingness" making itself noisy. The predictive speech of business tycoons and systems analysts without love brings nothing but harsh sounds upon our ears. The esoteric ramblings of witches, wizards, and seers may carry us aloft in our thoughts - but, without cups of water given to the thirsty it is entirely of no avail. The accumulation of facts and the compilation of data in the age of information is incredibly impressive. But, what good is it to be informed with information - if we cannot be shaped and formed "in love?"

Faith may remove mountains which obstruct our view or block our path. But, only love can heal the one who is overcome by sickness and despair of life. Only love can raise the one upon whom death's shadows has fallen.

Kahlil Gibran takes us into the unfathomable depths and the immeasurable reaches of love, with these verses:

> Love gives naught but itself and takes not from itself.
> Love possesses not nor would be possessed;
> For love is sufficient unto love.
>
> When you love you should not say, "God is in my heart," but rather, "I am in the heart of God." And think not you can direct the course of love, for love, if it finds you worthy, directs your course. (K. Gibran, *The Prophet. On Love*)

Thirteen

JOURNEY FOR THE LOVE OF GOD
A Compelling Quest

Jesus Walked this Lonesome Valley

Jesus walked this lonesome valley.
He had to walk it by himself:
O' nobody else could walk it for Him,
He had to walk it by himself.

We must walk this lonesome valley,
We have to walk it by ourselves:
O' nobody else can walk it for us,
We have to walk it by ourselves.

You must go and stand your trial,
You have to stand it by yourself,
O' nobody else can stand it for you,
You have to stand it by yourself.
(Traditional American Folk Hymn, based on Psalm 23:4)

The whole idea of life being a journey is basic to humanity. There are countless stories of individuals setting off on greatly compelling quests for knowledge and enlightenment, ecstasy and fulfillment. They venture out on what often become long journeys inspired by a dream or a vision. There is the medieval search for The Holy Grail, the ancient myths of the Odyssey, and the gallant knights who were summoned to the Holy Land during the crusades. History is replete with many stories of spiritual wanderings, and of exodus treks as pilgrims and saints are guided and sustained on their journey by God.

Those who have responded in the affirmative to Jesus Christ's call to follow him have given their allegiance to the wandering Saviour who said: "Foxes have holes, and birds of the air have their nests, but the Son of Man has nowhere to lay his head." (Matthew 8:20)

The early Christians were first called followers of The Way, before they were identified as "Christ-like" that is, "Christian." In her book, *The Celtic Way of Prayer*, Esther de Waal makes these comments:

> Jesus went into the wilderness for forty days like Moses and the children of Israel did for forty years. Our Saviour made his journey through life to death and Resurrection. That pattern of journeying is also our destiny.
>
> The journey will be difficult in some ways. It will also be surprising - not necessarily following some specific, predetermined "end or goal." (pg.1)

Jesus Christ was an adventurer. He left his parent's house and his home town area - everything which was familiar to him. He embarked on a journey defined by destiny and guided by providence. Jesus did not seem to be timid, afraid, or held back by self-questioning as he traveled along. He trusted God the Father to guide him each step of the way. His conception - his image of God was that of a loving, heavenly Father who was with him continually.

Jesus launched his mission to the world with single minded courage and determination. He boldly proclaimed to his people and nation that the kingdom of heaven was "breaking in" upon them. A radically new day was dawning upon them. A compelling, horizon of hope called out to Jesus as he left his childhood home in Nazareth. He moved forward in his mission and ministry always and in every place determined to accomplish the will of God. Jesus fully submitted himself to his calling to serve. He broke new ground with his straight forward declaration that he was "the way, the truth, and the life." (John 14:6)

Even though Jesus was very much involved with people on a daily basis, he nevertheless set himself apart from them as well. His singularity of mind and devotion of heart was entirely unique. He did not seem to be lonely in the way in which we understand loneliness – being emotionally deficient and unable to function properly. Jesus was alone in what he had been divinely appointed to do – alone in the way in which he intended to accomplish his divine mission.

Jesus was faithful to his calling from his earliest years. This is first clearly evidenced when he was twelve years of age. Joseph and Mary took him at that time to Jerusalem for the Feast of the Passover. They left the city when the festivities were over but Jesus stayed behind by himself without them knowing it. It took them three days to find him. When they found him they were annoyed – they did not understand why he had left them.

Here is Luke's account of the incident:

> They found Jesus in the Temple, sitting among the teachers, listening to them and asking them questions. And all who heard him were astonished at his understanding and his answers. When his parents saw him they were astonished; and his mother said to him, "Child, why have you treated us like this? Look, your father and I have been searching for you in great anxiety?" He said to them, "Why were you searching for me? Did you not know that I must be about my Father's

business?" But they did not understand what he said to them. (Luke 2:46-50)

"The Father's business" [God's] will be of prime concern to those who have chosen to be true followers of Jesus. They will be active in that which they consider to be God's purposes for the world. In that sense, they will be working to establish the Kingdom of Heaven upon earth. They will prove, champion, and defend all actions – theirs and that of others which promote and advance the Kingdom of God as it is believed to be coming from above and beyond the earth.

As with Jesus, the "business" of God will often cause his followers to act in new and extraordinary ways. They will do things which will seem unusual to the common mind – because they are motivated by what they consider to be the will of God. Issues of justice will compel them to speak and act against oppression and tyranny. Those who cruelly abuse weak, disadvantaged, and vulnerable persons will be called to account by fearless champions of the gospel. Inevitably, those who are followers of The Way of Christ will encounter rejection, ridicule, and opposition. They will, as in the past, be frequently disregarded, persecuted, and marginalized. Being faithful to Jesus Christ carries a cost – the disciple cannot expect to be treated any differently than the Master.

People of faith who wish to be "about" the heavenly Father's business in identification with The One who is called the Son of God, will find that they must entrust themselves to the Spirit of God for leading and guidance. Great spiritual works can only be accomplished in and by the power of the Spirit.

At times, there will be a certain randomness and unpredictability to the journey of faith. Those following the way of the gospel will not always know exactly where they are being led. Those embarking on the journey of faith will not be fully certain of their pathway or completely aware of their destination. The only thing that will be completely certain for them will be their belief and conviction that they are being guided by God.

There is the ancient story of three Irish monks who set out in a small boat called a coracle upon the Irish Sea. They drifted over the sea for seven days until they came ashore in Cornwall in the south of England. They were promptly brought into the court of King Alfred and ordered to stand before the King. He asked them where they had come from and where they were going. Their answer was simple and straight forward, "We stole away upon the Sea because we wanted, for the love of God to be on a pilgrimage - we cared not where or how."

The small boats used by the Irish monks of old were called coracles. Here is Webster's dictionary description of a coracle:

> A small boat used by fishermen made by covering a wicker frame with leather or oilcloth, being so light as to be easily carried. A similar boat was used by the ancient Egyptians.

The coracle was a boat without oars or a rudder. When it was being paddled along, it could easily be picked up by strong currents. The ancient monks' journey was a risky, perilous undertaking. They simply trusted God to direct them and accompany them as their little boat bounced along on top of the waves. We imagine them to have fully expected that the Spirit of God would hover over the waters of the sea - as on the first day of Creation. The story tells us that the monks' faith in God was sincere and ingenuous. They simply believed that God would "stir up" some good ocean currents for them. They entrusted their mission and their destiny in The One who had calmed the waters of the Sea of Galilee so long ago. Wind and wave would be obedient to the voice of Jesus, the miracle worker who, as it was told, had also come to his followers walking upon the surface of the waters of that same Sea.

The words of the prophet, Amos, come to mind:

> "Prepare to meet your God, O Israel. For lo, the One who forms the mountains, and creates the wind reveals his thoughts to mortal Man. He who treads on the heights of the earth - the Lord, the God of hosts, is his name." (4:13)

The Old Testament book of Exodus, as previously noted, records the story of a Hebrew mother who launched her little baby boy out onto the waters of the Nile River. Into a tiny coracle, a small ark made of bulrushes daubed with slime and pitch to make it watertight, his mother placed her little baby boy whom we know as Moses. He was a person of great destiny, in that he became the deliverer of the people of God from slavery in Egypt.

A mighty man of God was rescued from the waters – when he was a vulnerable infant. A son of destiny was threatened when he was a baby. But, waters of salvation, we could say, bore him along to just the right place where he could be rescued. An Egyptian princess felt sorry for little Moses who was crying when she first saw him. Moved by compassion, she took him out of the coracle and raised him in the household of the Pharaoh. Jochebed, the mother of Moses, didn't know what would happen to Moses when she pushed him out among the reeds in the river. Being a person of faith, she put her trust in God. Being a believer in divine providence, she gave herself and her child over into the will of God.

Moses was raised as an Egyptian. But, when he became a man his own people and heritage came to have first place in his heart. Eventually, with a series of mighty acts of God being accomplished at his hand and in his favour, Moses led the Israelites out of slavery and then journeyed with them to the Promised Land.

The Irish monks, in the story related above, sailed away from their homeland on "a pilgrimage for the love of God" not caring where or how they went. A pilgrimage usually has a specific "end or goal" – a journey is made along a prescribed "well-worn" path. The pilgrims make their journey to a specific, holy place where there is a cathedral, shrine, or relics of the saints. They travel on a feast day or during a time of fasting. The pilgrim's journey to places officially designated as sacred. Miracles may have at one time taken place in those locations. Angels may have made appearances. At some, it is reported that the Virgin Mary revealed herself to her devotees.

With such phenomenal things supposedly being manifest, holy places become attractive to certain persons. Pilgrim travelers to these specific, holy spots are hopeful that similar, wonderful things will occur for them.

There is another type of pilgrimage known as "peregrinatio." The word is from the Latin meaning "to travel or wander in strange lands." Peregrini pilgrims set out on their journeys stirred to do so by an inner prompting of the Spirit of God. They have a passionate, deeply soulful conviction that they must undertake what is essentially an inner journey. It is not as important to reach a goal or arrive at a destination - as it is - to experience God each step along the way.

Esther de Waal gives this description of the peregrini:

> They are ready to go wherever the Spirit might take them. Seeing themselves as guests of the world, what they are seeking, is the place of their Resurrection, the resurrected self, the true self in Christ, which is for all of us, our true home. The journey is undertaken for the love of Christ, who holds first place in their hearts. (*Celtic Way of Prayer*, pg. 2)

Peregrini travelers do not expect to find God "guaranteed to be" as it were, in a particular location. Certain places may have spiritual significance. But, the "peregrini" believe it is better to experience God's presence by chance than to seek for it at the end of a prescribed route or holy way. It is better to travel unprotected and vulnerable than to be obsessed with making oneself completely secure. Better to be cautious and hesitant than to be overtaken by obsessive fears over security. Better to be apprehensive than to be paralyzed by anxiety over safety. People of "peregrini faith" are not foolish or irrational. Their desire is simply to learn how to trust The Presence which is unseen for guidance and protection. They place their faith in The Spirit which is above all and in all - but cannot be seen, touched, or handled.

Verses from the book of Proverbs come to mind: Trust in the Lord with all your heart, and do not rely on your own insight. In all your ways acknowledge him, and he will make straight your paths. (3:5, 6). Also, in the book of Hebrews, we have this related verse:

"Now faith is the assurance of things hoped for, the conviction of things not seen." (11:1)

The saints of God, who frequently experience the presence of The Holy One in many and varied places, tell us that God can be known in every place imaginable. The visionary mystics who claim to have ascended to the heavens, at certain times, tell us that God can be known in every second, minute, and hour of each day. Certain ardent followers of Jesus Christ testify, using the words of the popular hymn, In the Garden, that – "He walks with me (them) and he talks with me, and he tells me I am his own."

Faithful people of The Spirit, who helps them to wander where they believe they are supposed to wander, do not always know exactly where they are going or how. They simply have the assurance that they are moving in the right direction.

We remember some often quoted words of Jesus Christ:

> "Do not marvel that I said to you, You must be born [guided] from above. The wind blows where it wills and you hear the sound of it, but you do not know where it comes from, or, where it is going; so it is with every one who is born [led by] [of] the Spirit." (John 3:8)

The challenge before us is this – to be loving people of a loving God, The Holy One, who sees each little sparrow that falls to the ground and also takes careful note of astronauts landing on the moon.

May our "sojourning" upon this earth and through the lives which we are given from above – be continually blessed, guided, and sustained by The Love that is infinite, eternal, and unchanging.

††††††

Listen to me, you that pursue righteousness, you that seek the Lord. Look to the rock from which you were hewn, and the quarry from which you were dug. Look to Abraham your Father and to

Sarah who bore you; for he was but one when I called him, but I blessed him and made him many. Lift up your eyes to the heavens, and look at the earth beneath. My salvation will be forever, and my deliverance will never be ended.

Isaiah 51:1-2, 6

Fourteen

CONTEMPLATION OF AN INFINITE GLORY
Auschwitz Defied

He's Got The Whole World

He's got the whole world in His hand,
He's got the big, round world in His hand,
He's got the whole world in His hand,
He's got the whole world in His hand.

He's got the wind and the rain in His hand,
He's got the sun and the moon in His hand,
He's got the wind and the rain in His hand,
He's got the whole world in His hand.

He's got the little bitsy baby in His hand,
He's got the tiny little baby in His hand,
He's got the little bitsy baby in His hand,
He's got the whole world in His hand.

He's got you and me, brother, in His hand,
He's got you and me, sister, in His hand,
He's got you and me, brother, in His hand,
He's got the whole world in His hand.

He's got everybody in His hand,
He's got everybody in His hand,
He's got everybody in His hand,
He's got the whole world in His hand.
(Traditional African American Spiritual)

Our lives are essentially a gift from God. We do not choose to be born. We are given life. It comes from beyond – out of the mystery and wonder of God's will, purpose, and divine being. That which is from above and beyond in God comes wondrously near as God infuses life, vitality, and the divine presence into everything which exists.

The Apostle Paul gave some enlightened instruction to the Greeks of Athens, Greece concerning the nature of God and the mystery of life:

> The God who made the world and everything in it, he who is Lord of heaven and earth does not live in shrines made by human hands, nor is he served by human hands, as though he needed anything, since he himself gives to all mortals life and breath and all things. From one ancestor he made all nations to inhabit the whole earth, and he allotted the times of their existence and the boundaries of the places where they would live, so that they would search for God and perhaps grope for him and find him – though indeed he is not far from each one of us. For "In him we live and move and have our being;" as even some of your poets have said, "For we too are his offspring." (Acts 17: 24-28)

As already stated, if we view life and the world as truly a gift from God, we will be immensely thankful for everything. We will wake up in the morning with a sense of profound joy in our hearts. In addition, if we think of life and the world as given to us by God – out from that which infinitely above and beyond, we will be conscious of the divine presence influencing everything which exists. We will be continually aware of the ways in which the Spirit of God penetrates and permeates all of Creation.

In his book, Tides *and Seasons - Modern prayers in the Celtic Tradition*, David Adam states that the early Celtic Christians "sought to build an outer world which reflected their belief in the Presence and Oneness of God." (pg.x)

Along these lines, we have the following ancient affirmation of faith attributed to St. Patrick:

> Our God is the God of all men the God of heaven and
> earth the God of sea, of river, of sun and moon, and stars
> of the lofty mountains, and the lowly valleys.
> The God above heaven
> The God under heaven
> The God in heaven.
> He has his dwelling round heaven
> and earth and sea, and all that is in them.
> He inspires all
> He quickens all
> He dominates al,
> He sustains all.
> He lights the light of the sun.
> He furnishes the light of light.

The Holy Scriptures are the written Word of God - thoroughly able to instruct us in divine truth and guide us into responsive faith. We approach the Bible with gratitude. We pour over its pages thankful for the wondrous teaching contained therein. We are greatly enlightened, encouraged and lifted up in our spirits as the Scriptures "take root" within our minds, hearts, and souls.

In our appreciation of the Scriptures as foundational to our beliefs and precious to our practice of faith, we remember these verses from the Psalms:

> The Law of the Lord is perfect. The decrees of the
> Lord are sure. The precepts of the Lord are right. The
> commandment of the Lord is clear. The ordinances of the
> Lord are true. More to be desired are they than gold, even

much fine gold, sweeter also than honey and drippings of the honeycomb. (Psalm 19: 7-10)

If we love what we have been given in the Scriptures, they will strongly influence us towards faith in The One whom we Christians believe is the Saviour of the world. The intention of all Scripture is to gently but compellingly draw us to Jesus Christ. The ultimate expression of God's nature, the truest revelation of divine truth, and the greatest manifestation of the love of God is found in Jesus Christ.

The Apostle John speaks eloquently of the greatness of the gift that comes to us in Jesus Christ - the Word of God incarnate in human flesh:

> In the beginning was the Word, and the Word was with God, and the Word was God. He was in the beginning with God. All things came into being through him, and without him not one thing came into being. What has come into being him was life, and the life was the light of all people. The light shines in the darkness, and the darkness did not overcome it. (John 1:1-5)

This incredibly profound passage lends itself to a multiplicity of meaning and interpretation by those who translate its words and phrases. Here is how it is presented in The New English Bible:

> When all things began, the Word already was. The Word dwelt with God, and what God was, the Word was. The Word, then, was with God at the beginning, and through him all things came to be; no single thing was created without him. All that came to be - was alive with his life, and that life was the light of men. The light shines in the dark, and the dark has never mastered it.

Often, it is in our darkest hours that we become most aware of the unfailing light of God. We become aware of the presence of God when there is little to comfort us. We are surprisingly intimate with God when others shun us and cast us off. We experience the presence of that which is infinitely beyond and above when the world seems to be nothing but hard stones and useless dust beneath our feet.

Dr. Viktor E. Frankl (1905-97), was a famous psychotherapist, honoured and esteemed as President of the Austrian Medical Society. Frankl's unique contribution to his profession was in what is known as logotherapy - a therapy based on the concept of "the logos." Logos is a Greek word commonly defined as verbal and non verbal expression and communication wherein the speaker is united with that which is spoken. In the concept of "logos" there is an authenticity of truth which is unmistakable.

Dr. Frankl put forward the following explanation to explain what is meant by "logotherapy:"

> Logos is a Greek word that denotes "meaning." Logotherapy focuses on the meaning of human existence as well as on man's search for such a meaning. According to logotherapy, the striving to find a meaning in one's life is the primary motivational force in man.
> (Frankl, *Man's Search for Meaning*, pg. 153)

Logos is the Greek word used in the gospel of John, chapter 1, for Jesus Christ as The Word. Logos in that context, encompasses the idea of meaning and purpose - as it relates to God and to human life. Ultimate meaning has its origin in the being and nature of God. Creation itself is shaped and formed in and by an ultimate purpose. Life issues forth from the Eternal One in whom it originates and is contained.

Light is inextricably "part and parcel" of life - we cannot live without it. God dwells in eternal Light and as God's heart is a heart of love - whatever we know to be dark and foreboding, threatening and over against life and goodness is subject to the overarching rule of God. Darkness is doomed to fail, we could say. In fact, we know that it has never been completely successful in over powering and obliterating Light. It has always failed because it is, in a certain sense, fundamentally unreal. It is nothing but an opposite to that which is true. It is defined only as the absence of Light. It does not exist except when Light is withdrawn. However, as we shall illustrate next, when Light is absent, God is still present. There can never be a place, or any form of existence, which is completely separate or apart from God - the ruler of all, the originator of all, the transcendent being in whom everything exists and has its reality.

Viktor Frankl insisted that mental and emotional health can only be obtained through "the will to meaning." Frankl did not derive his method from scholarly books or with the help of other learned persons. His unique approach to psychotherapy arose out of his own personal experience.

Frankl spent three years as a prisoner at Auschwitz and other Nazi concentration camps during the Second World War. He gained freedom only to learn that almost his entire family had been wiped out. It was during and partly because of the incredible suffering and degradation of those terrible years that Frankl was able to develop his theory and practice of logotherapy. It is a truly remarkable and appealing approach to the human dilemma with its insistence that meaning can be found in all forms of human experience even the most brutal and horrific. We discover for ourselves - or, are given from outside ourselves, some meaning for our lives. It may be small or fragile but it is enough for us. We continue to live. We do not die. Hope enlivens our souls. We find, we are given, we discover - how we can successfully sustain ourselves in the life which we have known.

Viktor Frankl believed that we are primarily and existentially driven by a striving to find meaning and purpose for living. Without a sense of meaning we can easily be overcome by a crippling sense of boredom, apathy, emptiness, and futility. With a sense of meaning motivating us and strengthening us, we are able to live psychologically healthy lives. It is also a crucial requirement that we be able to survive painful experiences. According to Frankl, the Holocaust survivor, life can have meaning and significance even in the midst of absurd, painful, and dehumanizing situations. Suffering itself has meaning. Frankl is quoted as having said, "What is to give light must endure burning."

In his book, *Man's Search for Meaning*, Frankl writes about how under the terrible conditions endured in the concentration camps some of the prisoners were able to keep alive and even deepen a spiritual life. They were able to retreat from their terrible surroundings into a life of "inner riches and spiritual freedom."

Here is an account of an early morning march of the prisoners to their work site:

> We stumbled on in the darkness along the road leading from the camp - the guards shouting at us and driving us with the butts of their rifles. Hardly a word was spoken; the icy wind did not encourage talk. Holding his mouth behind his collar, the man next to me whispered: "If only our wives could see us now! I do hope they are better off in their camps and don't know what is happening to us."
>
> That brought thoughts of my own wife to mind. As we stumbled on for miles, nothing was said but we both knew each of us was thinking of his wife. My mind was fixed on my wife's image. I heard her answering me, saw her smile, her frank and encouraging look. Real or not, her look was then more luminous than the sun which was rising.
>
> A thought transfixed me. Love is the ultimate and highest goal to which we can aspire. Salvation is through love and in love. Someone who has nothing left in this world may still know bliss, if only for a brief moment, in the contemplation of his beloved. I understood the meaning of the words, "The angels are lost in perpetual contemplation of an infinite glory." (*The Will to Meaning*, pgs. 57-58)

There is an infinite glory to be found in Creation because the Creator is infinitely wonderful and glorious. We need only look around us at any given moment and our minds take pause - we are overwhelmed and amazed with the beauty of the wonders we behold. In the Psalms we read:

The heavens are telling the glory of God; the firmament
proclaims his handiwork. Day to day fours forth speech
and night to night declares knowledge. (Psalm 19:1, 2)

There is an infinite wonder and glory to be found in the Saviour,
Jesus Christ, who is described by one gospel song writer as:

The lily of the valley, the bright and morning star,
The fairest of ten thousand to my soul.
(*The Lily of the Valley*, Charles W. Fry, 1881)

The Apostle John was the disciple reputed to be the most intimate
with Jesus Christ. In the following passage, he gives us an account
of the incredible impact which Jesus had on those who actually
experienced his presence with and among them:

And the Word was made flesh, and dwelt among us, and
we beheld his glory, the glory as of the only begotten of
the Father, full of grace and truth. (John 1:14, KJV)

Our lives will reflect the radiance of God as we believe in and
faithfully follow Jesus Christ as Lord and Saviour. God's grandeur
is reflected in us as we humbly ascribe – all that we do – to the
glory of God. Our "will to meaning" found in God and in Christ
overcomes the darkness, degradation, and despair of our world. Our
dark, cloudy days are lit up by the resplendent wonders of creation,
and the divinely, incarnated radiance of God in Jesus Christ, because:
"The Holy Ghost (the Spirit of God) over the bent world broods with
warm breast and ah! bright wings." (Poem, *God's Grandeur*. Gerald
Manley Hopkins)

The sweet delight to which we are born may be minimal for
many of us – if we understand it only in terms of long lasting joys
and greatly satisfying experiences. Some of us are given much more
of this world's goods and pleasures than others. Some truly good
people deserve to receive a much greater blessing than what they
actually receive. Life is not fair in many ways, to be sure. We cannot

deny the appalling injustice which is experienced by so many. "Evil rears its ugly head" continually. Its oppressive manifestations heap untold suffering upon millions. In this day and age, Mother Earth is threatened as never before. Changes occurring on the surface of the earth and in the skies above fill us with fear and foreboding. We wonder, "How much time is left for us to live – as we have been living?"

In each moment of time given to us, remembering the words of William Blake's with which we began our study, let us trust as best we are able, that God will come to us – in whatever circumstance we find ourselves.

Some are born to sweet delight.
God appears & God is Light

May each morning that comes, whether it be with bright, radiant sunshine and not a cloud in the sky – or, with dark clouds, storms, and heavy rain – nevertheless bring with it some large or small manifestation of Light from above – so that we, as much as we able, may truly "dwell in realms of day."

O, Brothers, Don't Get Weary

O, brothers, don't get weary,
O, brothers, don't get weary,
O, brothers, don't get weary,
We're waiting for the Lord.

We'll land on Canaan's shore,
We'll land on Canaan's shore,
When we land on Canaan's shore
We'll meet forevermore.
(African American Spiritual)

BIBLIOGRAPHY

Adam, David. *Tides and Seasons, Modern Prayers in the Celtic Tradition.* Triangle SPCK, London, 1989.

Best Loved Negro Spirituals. Compiled, Edited, N.B. Herder. Dover Publications, Mineola, New York, 2001.

Blake, William. *Everyman's Poetry.* Collins, New York, 1997.

Bonhoeffer, Dietrich. *Letters and Papers from Prison.* Collins Fontana Books, 1964.

Book of Praise, Revised 1972. The Presbyterian Church in Canada. Don Mills. Ontario.

Brown, Robert McAffee. Gutierrez, Gustavo, *An Introduction to Liberation Theology.* Orbis Books, Mary Knoll, New York, 1990.

College Survey of English Literature. Revised, Shorter Edition. ed. A.M. Witherspoon. Harcourt, Brace, New York, 1951.

Confession of Faith, Westminster: for Presbyterian Publications, Toronto. Wm. Blackwood, Edinburgh, 1957.

De Waal, Esther. *Celtic Way of Prayer.* Image Books, Doubleday, New York, 1997.

Fox, Matthew. *Creation Spirituality: Liberating Gifts for the Peoples of the Earth.* Harper, San Francisco, 1991.

Frankl, Victor E. *Man's Search for Meaning, An Introduction to Logotherapy.* Washington Square Press, New York, 1963.

Gibran, Kahlil. *The Prophet.* Alfred A. Knopf. 1997.

Gutierrez, Gustavo. *On Job – God-Talk and the Suffering of the Innocent.* Orbis, New York, 1989.

Kabbalah, *The Essential: The Heart of Jewish Mysticism.* Daniel C. Matt. Castle Books. New Jersey, 1997.

Modern Poetry, Vol. VII. ed. Mack, Dean and Frost. Prentice Hall, Englewood Cliffs, N.J. 1963.

Morris, Leon. *Gospel According to John. The New International Commentary.* Eeerdmans Publishing, Michigan, 1975.

O'Donohue, John. *To Bless The Space Between Us, A Book of Blessings.* Double Day, New York, 2008.

Rylaarsdam, J.C. *Proverbs to Song of Solomon. Layman's Bible Commentary.* SCM Press, London, 1964.

The Pattern of our Days, Worship in the Celtic Tradition from the Iona Community. ed. Kathy Galloway. Paulist Press. New York.

Touchstones, Daily Meditations for Men. Hazelden Educational Materials, Minnesota, Date unknown.

Von Rad, Gerhard. *Genesis, A Commentary. The Old Testament Library,* Westminster Press, Philadelphia, 1961.

ABOUT THE AUTHOR

John Barry Forsyth is an ordained Presbyterian Minister. He has served congregations in British Columbia, Ontario, Nova Scotia, and Quebec in Canada. John Barry has degrees in history, education, and theology. At various times, he has been a teacher, counsellor, triathlete, and competitive swimmer.

Printed in the United States
By Bookmasters